The Article Book

Practice Toward Mastering
a, *an*, and *the*

T O M   C O L E

American Language & Cultural Institute
Arizona State University

PRENTICE HALL REGENTS
A VIACOM COMPANY
Upper Saddle River, NJ 07458

Publisher: Mary Jane Peluso
Development Editor: Carol Callahan
Production Editor: Noël Vreeland Carter
Interior design: Paula Williams
Manufacturing: Ray Keating
Art Director: Merle Krumper
Interior Art: Daniel Baxter
Cover Design: Bruce Kenselaar

PRENTICE HALL REGENTS
A VIACOM COMPANY

© 1997 by Prentice Hall Regents
Prentice-Hall, Inc.
A Simon & Schuster Company
Upper Saddle River, NJ   07458

Printed in the United States of America

10 9 8 7 6 5 4 3 2 1

ISBN 0-13-311390-6

Prentice Hall International (UK) Limited, London
Prentice Hall of Australia Pty. Limited, Sydney
Prentice Hall Canada, Inc., Toronto
Prentice Hall Hispanoamericana, S.A., Mexico
Prentice Hall of India Private Limited, New Delhi
Prentice Hall of Japan, Inc., Tokyo
Simon & Schuster Asia Pte. Ltd., Singapore
Editora Prentice Hall do Brasil, Ltda., Rio de Janeiro

To my mom and dad

 # CONTENTS

CHAPTER THREE

PART E

CHAPTER FOUR

PART F

CHAPTER FIVE

PART G

PART H

CHAPTER SIX

PART I

PART J

APPENDIX

█INTRODUCTION

To the Student

How to Learn with *THE ARTICLE BOOK*

There is a a lot to learn in *The Article Book*. Here's how:

✓ First, start at the beginning. Even if you are an advanced student, you will learn more if you do. The chapters of the book <u>can</u> be studied in any order, but you will understand more if you work through the chapters in order.

✓ Second, use the glossary in the back of the book. If you do not understand a word, use the glossary to find an explanation. This will make studying *The Article Book* much easier.

✓ Third, spend enough time on each chapter. There is a lot of practice in the book, but it takes time to feel comfortable using articles in English. After you finish a chapter, read it again. Then, look in other English books for examples like the ones you have studied. Write some sentences of your own that are similar to the practice sentences.

✓ Fourth, remember that NO RULES ARE ABSOLUTE. The rules in *The Article Book* are only useful guides. You should not try to memorize them. You will learn much more from the exercises and readings in the book than from the rules themselves.

✓ Finally, use your book when you write or do other work in English—the same way you use your dictionary. *The Article Book* is a reference that you can use every day.

To the Teacher

What is *THE ARTICLE BOOK*

The Article Book is meant to be both a comprehensive guide and workbook for improving students' understanding of English articles—*an*, *an*, and *the*. While many texts include segments on article use, the presentation is usually too superficial to help students build confidence when using these often confusing words. *The Article Book* has been written with the intent of filling that gap. At the same time, it provides useful readings, grammar, and vocabulary.

The Article Book first teaches the basic and most common elements of article use. As students progress through the book, they are introduced to more advanced and less common use of articles. There are 50 rules and 15 exceptions, but learning takes place principally through guided practice. The rules exist primarily to provide a logical framework for the text and to serve as a handy reference. Students are instructed not to try to memorize them.

Acknowledgments

I owe thanks to Gailynn Valdés for her interest and encouragement in the development of this book and to Wendy Vicens who reviewed my early draft and set me on the right track. I am also indebted to Nancy Baxer who first suggested I begin a text on articles.

The Article Book

CHAPTER ONE

Read the rules for Part A and study the examples. Do not try to memorize the rules. Instead, do the exercises that follow the rules.

Rule 1: Use *a* when a singular count noun is indefinite and the article is followed by a consonant sound.

Do you have a pen?
There is a dirt road at the north end of this town.
Mr. Green bought a used car.

NOTE: Indefinite means not already known, not already understood, or not already mentioned.

Rule 2: Use *an* when a singular count noun is indefinite and the article is followed by a vowel sound.

Do you have an umbrella?
Is there an eraser in your desk?
He is an honorable man.

NOTE: It is not the letter but the sound that determines whether *a* or *an* should be used. Words that begin with the letters *eu* (as in *Europe*) or the letter *u* (as in *use*) sometimes have the sound you hear at the beginning of the word *you* when you say it.

EXERCISE A1

Write *a* or *an* in the space.

1. Could you tell me where I can find _____ good restaurant in this town?

2. Sure. There's _____ place on Fifth Street that serves great Mexican food. It's _____ excellent restaurant.

3. Is it _____ easy walk from here?

4. Yes, about five minutes. It's right next to _____ used book store.

ANSWERS: 1. a 2. a, an 3. an 4. a

EXERCISE A2

Write *a* or *an* in the spaces.

1. _____ ugly color   2. _____ united country   3. _____ unfinished poem

ANSWERS: 1. an 2. a 3. an

Which of the above words begins with the sound you hear at the beginning of the word *you*?

ANSWER: united

EXERCISE A3

Write *a* or *an* in the spaces.

1. _____ early class
2. _____ engine
3. _____ European country

ANSWERS: 1. an 2. an 3. a

Which of the above words begins with the sound you hear at the beginning of the word *you?*

_____

ANSWER: European

Write *a* or *an* in the spaces.

1. _____ home
2. _____ hot dog
3. _____ hour

ANSWERS: 1. a 2. a 3. an

Sometimes the letter *h* is not pronounced. Say the three words above that begin with *h.* In which of the words in the *h* silent? _____

ANSWER: hour

PUTTING IT TOGETHER

Pronounce each word softly. Write *a* or *an* in the spaces.

1. _____ honorable judge
2. _____ unusual story
3. _____ hour
4. _____ useful book
5. _____ honest person
6. _____ university
7. _____ horse
8. _____ used car
9. _____ European
10. _____ house
11. _____ uniform
12. _____ ear

ANSWERS: 1. an 2. an 3. an 4. a 5. an 6. a 7. a 8. a 9. a 10. a 11. a 12. an

Read the following rules and study the examples.

> **Rule 3: Do not use *a* or *an* with plural nouns.**
>
> Correct: I have brothers and sisters in Australia.
> Correct: There are automobiles in the parking lot.
>
> Incorrect: I have a brothers and sisters in Australia.
> Incorrect: There are an automobiles in the parking lot.

> **Rule 4: Do not use *a* or *an* with noncount nouns.**
>
> Correct: I drank milk yesterday.
> Correct: We need oxygen to breathe.
>
> Incorrect: I drank a milk yesterday.
> Incorrect: We need an oxygen to breathe.

EXERCISE A4

Complete the sentences with noncount nouns. Do not use articles.

pepper   money   food   tea   air   coffee   water

1. People need _____ to breathe and _____ to drink.
2. In the U.S. _____ is a more popular drink than _____.
3. I want to buy a house, so I need _____.
4. We're hungry! We want _____!
5. I like salt, but I don't like _____ because it makes me sneeze.

ANSWERS: 1. air, water 2. coffee, tea 3. money 4. food 5. pepper

✔ Quick Check

Check the INCORRECT sentences.

❏ 1. A cats are popular pets.
❏ 2. This book is made of a paper.
❏ 3. Lions eat a meat.
❏ 4. An automobiles cause pollution.
❏ 5. Cheese is made from milk.

ANSWERS: 1, 2, 3, 4 (Number 5 is correct.)

Now write the INCORRECT parts of the sentences correctly.

1. _Cats_ _____
2. _____
3. _____
4. _____

ANSWERS: 2. paper 3. meat 4. automobliles

PUTTING IT TOGETHER

Write the correct article in each space. If no article is needed, write ø.

1. _____ Calorie is _____ unit of _____ heat.
2. _____ snow and _____ ice are forms of _____ water.
3. _____ European cars are usually _____ good machines.
4. _____ glass is made from _____ sand.
5. It is _____ honor to have _____ university degree.

ANSWERS: 1. A, a, ø 2. ø, ø, ø 3. ø, ø 4. ø, ø 5. an, a

3

Read the following rules and study the examples.

Rule 5: **Do not use *the* with indefinite nouns.**

> Correct: She likes to drink milk.
> Correct: Do you have brothers and sisters?
> Incorrect: She likes to drink the milk.
> Incorrect: Do you have the brothers and sisters?

Rule 6: **Do not use *the* with *there* + "be." (All nouns, plural and singular, are indefinite if they occur after *there* + "be.")**

> Correct: There is a pen on the table.
> Correct: There were planes in the sky.
> Incorrect: There is the pen on the table.
> Incorrect: There were the planes in the sky.

EXERCISE A5

Write the correct article in the space. If no article is needed, write ø.

> ### The Great Basin Desert
>
> There is _____ wonderful place that I visit on _____ holidays. It is _____ desert.
> ₁ ... ₂ ... ₃
> _____ people usually think that _____ deserts are hot, but it is not _____ heat that makes
> ₄ ... ₅ ... ₆
> _____ desert but the absence of _____ water. This desert has _____ cold winter. I like to
> ₇ ... ₈ ... ₉
> go there because it is such _____ quiet and peaceful place. There is _____ white sand
> ₁₀ ... ₁₁
> everywhere, and in the distance there are _____ beautiful mountains covered with _____
> ₁₂ ... ₁₃
> snow. I can think of no other place I would rather be.

ANSWERS: 1. a. 2. ø 3. a 4. ø 5. ø 6. ø 7. a 8. ø 9. a 10. a 11. ø 12. ø 13. ø

✔ Quick Check

Check the INCORRECT sentences.

- ❑ 1. Do you often drink the orange juice?
- ❑ 2. My car uses a gasoline.
- ❑ 3. Paper was invented by the Chinese.
- ❑ 4. Blood is red.
- ❑ 5. Some beaches in Hawaii have the black sand.

ANSWERS: 1, 2, 5 (Numbers 3 and 4 are correct.)

Now write the incorrect parts of the sentences correctly (without an article).

1. _____orange juice_____   2. _____   5. _____
ANSWERS: 2. gasoline 5. black sand

Articles in Context

Read the story carefully. Then read the questions and complete the answers.

An Easy Airplane to Fly

3 An airplane is a useful machine, but most people can't afford to buy one. That's why the "Very EZ" was invented. You don't buy a Very EZ; you build it from plans. It takes about a year to build one.

6 A Very EZ is an unusual plane because of its wings. There is a wing in the middle of the plane and one in front. There are also seats for two people. People like these airplanes because

9 they are safe and easy to fly and they don't waste fuel.

"I finished my Very EZ last year," says John Filmore, a private pilot from Sandpoint, Idaho.

12 It's an excellent plane and very economical. I can fly from my home to California without running out of gasoline. My plane is also quite safe. I know it is because I built it myself!"

Is an airplane useful?	Yes, it's _____ useful machine.
Is a Very EZ a regular airplane?	No, it's _____ unusual one.
Do people buy these planes?	No, they build them from _____ plans.
How many people can fly in one?	There are _____ seats for two.
What's in the front of the plane?	There is _____ wing in front.
Why are they economical?	They don't waste _____ fuel.
Who is John Filmore?	He's _____ private pilot.
What does he say about the plane?	He says it's _____ excellent plane.
Does John's plane use much gas?	No, when he flies to California from his home
	he still has _____ gasoline when he lands.

Quiz 1

Write *a* or *an* in the space provided. If no article is needed, write ø in the space. Then check your answers in the back of the book.

1. It takes me _____ hour to get to school from my house.

2. My father doesn't drink coffee, but he does drink _____ tea.

3. Photos show that there is _____ tremendous canyon on Mars.

4. I have an aunt and _____ uncle in Korea.

5. Many men hate _____ ties.

5

BEYOND THE RULES

Some nouns can be count nouns in some instances and noncount nouns in others.
Write the correct article in the space. If no article is needed, write ø.

1. Einstein developed a theory regarding space and _____ time.
2. We had _____ great time at the beach last week.
3. The waiter brought me _____ glass of water.
4. Look out! I broke a bottle and there's _____ glass on the floor!

ANSWERS: 1. ø 2. a 3. a 4. ø

Some noncount nouns can appear with *a* or *an* if the meaning is "a kind of."
Write the correct article in the space. If no article is needed, write ø.

1. The pilot ran out of _____ fuel and had to land in a field.
2. Gasoline is _____ fuel made from petroleum.
3. Red Mountain is _____ inexpensive wine.
4. _____ wine is an alcoholic beverage.

ANSWERS: 1. ø 2. a 3. an 4. ø

Look at sentences 2 and 3 above and complete the following.

2. _____ is _____ kind of fuel _____.
3. _____ is an _____ kind of wine.

ANSWERS: 2. Gasoline is a kind of fuel made from petroleum. 3. Red Mountain is an inexpensive kind of wine.

PUTTING IT TOGETHER

Write *a* or ø in each space.

1. After the accident, there was _____ glass in the street.
2. A crow is much smarter than _____ chicken.
3. I'm tired of the meals at my sister's house. She always serves _____ chicken.
4. Longhorn is _____ yellow Cheddar cheese.
5. A cheeseburger has _____ cheese, and a hamburger doesn't.
6. I hope you have _____ wonderful time on vacation.

ANSWERS: 1. ø 2. a 3. ø 4. a 5. ø 6. a

NOTE: Number 4 takes *a* because not all yellow cheese is Longhorn. Longhorn is just one kind of yellow Cheddar cheese.

Comprehensive Test 1

Write *the*, *a*, or *an* in the space provided. If no article is needed, write ø in the space. Then check your answers in the back of the book.

1. There is _____ interesting movie playing at the Valley Art Theater.

2. She lives in a place where there are _____ long cold winters.

3. The Air Bus is made by _____ European company.

4. What _____ honor it is to meet you!

5. I saw _____ horrible accident on the highway last week.

6. The police often call _____ unknown man "John Doe."

7. _____ whales breathe air.

8. Everything went wrong; we had _____ terrible time.

9. _____ time and space are related.

10. Wait a minute; I've got _____ idea!

11. Do you have _____ driver's license?

12. The State Press is _____ university newspaper.

13. Some people say that _____ money is the source of all evil.

14. The hungry are asking for _____ bread.

15. Is _____ grapefruit juice a popular drink in your country?

16. _____ pig is an intelligent animal.

17. I don't really like _____ pork.

18. India ink is _____ special kind of ink.

19. My pen is out of _____ ink.

20. There are _____ penguins in Antarctica but not at the North Pole.

Part B

Read the rules for Part B and study the examples. Do not try to memorize the rules. Instead, do the exercises that follow the rules.

Rule 7: **Use _a_ for single letters and numbers that begin with a consonant sound.**

John got a "B" on his history test.
The professor wrote a "2" on the board.

Rule 8: **Use _an_ for letters and numbers that begin with a vowel sound.**

Mary got an "A" on her geology test.
The math teacher wrote an "8" on the board.

EXERCISE B1

Say the letters of the alphabet. Then write _a_ or _an_ in the space.

_____ A	_____ B	_____ C	_____ D	_____ E	_____ F
_____ G	_____ H	_____ I	_____ J	_____ K	_____ L
_____ M	_____ N	_____ O	_____ P	_____ Q	_____ R
_____ S	_____ T	_____ U	_____ V	_____ W	_____ X
_____ Y	_____ Z				

ANSWERS: All take _a_ except _a, e, f, h, i, l, m, n, o, r, s,_ and _x,_ which take _an._

_____ 1	_____ 2	_____ 3	_____ 4	_____ 5	_____ 6
_____ 7	_____ 8	_____ 9	_____ 10	_____ 11	_____ 12
_____ 13	_____ 14	_____ 15	_____ 16	_____ 17	_____ 18
_____ 30	_____ 40	_____ 50	_____ 60	_____ 70	_____ 80

ANSWERS: All take _a_ except 8, 11, 18, and 80, which take _an._

✔ Quick Check

Check the INCORRECT sentences.

❏ 1. I wrote a "8" on the board.
❏ 2. My name begins with a "L."
❏ 3. A "98" is a very high grade.
❏ 4. "Henry" begins with a "H."

ANSWERS: 1, 2, 4 (Number 3 is correct.)

Now write the incorrect parts of the sentences correctly.

1. _an "8"_ 　　　　2. _____ 　　　　4. _____

ANSWERS: 2. _an_ "L" 4. _an_ "H"

Read the following rules and study the examples.

Rule 9: Use *a* to mean "for each" or "per" when the noun begins with a consonant sound.

> Eggs are only 79 cents a dozen.
> My car gets 26 miles a gallon.

Rule 10: Use *an* to mean "for each" or "per" when the noun begins with a vowel sound.

> An airliner can travel more than 600 miles an hour.
> This perfume costs 300 dollars an ounce.

EXERCISE B2

Write *a* or *an* in the space.

1. The speed limit on this highway is sixty-five miles _____ hour.
2. Land here costs $30,000 _____ acre.
3. This gold chain sells for $40.00 _____ inch.
4. People in this company typically work forty hours _____ week.

ANSWERS: 1. an 2. an 3. an 4. a

Articles in Context

Read the following story carefully and answer the questions. Then read the story again to check your answers.

Masahiro Matsubara

Masahiro Matsubara is an unusually talented and intelligent young man. At the age of 15, he
3 can throw an 85-mile-an-hour fastball and is the pitcher for his school's baseball team. He can also hit the ball well. Masahiro averages two
6 home runs a game.

You might think that baseball is Masahiro's whole life, but it isn't everything to him.
9 "Sports aren't the most important thing to me," he says. "I was really unhappy when I got a "B" in English last semester. I was doing all right in that class until I got a "70" on the final exam. Good grades mean a lot to me and only
12 getting a "B" really hurt. "I'm getting an "A" this semester."

How fast is Masahiro's fast ball?	About 85 miles _____ hour
Can he make home runs?	Yes, he averages two _____ game.
Are sports everything to him?	No, _____ good grades are more important.
What made Masahiro unhappy?	He got _____ "B" in his English class.
How did he do on the final exam?	He got _____ "70."
What does he want to do?	He wants to get _____ "A" next time.

 **Quiz 2**

Write *a* or *an* in the space provided. If no article is needed, write ø in the space. Then, check your answers in the back of the book.

1. The teacher wrote _____ "11" on the board.
2. The word "hatch" has _____ "H" at the beginning and at the end.
3. When I was in college, I had a job that paid $1.60 _____ hour.
4. Gold used to sell for thirty-five dollars _____ ounce.
5. I feed my dog twice _____ day.

Part C

Read the rules for Part C and study the examples. Do not try to memorize the rules. Instead, do the exercises that follow the rules.

> **Rule 11: Use *the* with *in the morning, in the afternoon,* and *in the evening.***
>
> In the morning, I usually have fruit, cereal, and milk.
> Classes are held in the afternoon.
> Professor Smith studies in the evening.

> **Rule 12: Do not use an article for *at night.***
>
> Correct: I often watch television at night.
>
> Incorrect: I often watch television at the night.

EXERCISE C1

Write ø or *the* in the space.

1. My father comes home from work at five o'clock in _____ afternoon.
2. In _____ morning, I am often awakened by birds singing.
3. The stars come out at _____ night.
4. Many people like to read in _____ evening.
5. Even fish sleep at _____ night.

ANSWERS: 1. the 2. the 3. ø 4. the 5. ø

Rule 13: Use *the* when the noun has already been mentioned.

I saw a dog. The dog ran away.
Some planes appeared. The planes landed in a field.

EXERCISE C2

Write *the* in the space if the noun that follows has already been mentioned.

1. The doctor treated a patient. _____ patient got well.
2. I planted a garden. _____ garden grew.
3. The mailman put some letters in the box. _____ letters were for me.
4. Mr. Burroughs wrote a book. _____ book was *Tarzan of the Apes*.
5. I caught a train in Tokyo, but I was late because _____ train broke down.
6. Most people like butterflies but hate _____ spiders.

ANSWERS: 1. the 2. the 3. the 4. the 5. the 6. ø Note: In number 6, the word *spiders* has not been
mentioned before.

BEYOND THE RULES

The word *some* can be used for indefinite noncount and indefinite plural nouns. It indicates an unspecified quantity or number. It is usually <u>optional</u>.

Write *some* or ø in the space if the sentence refers to quantity or number. If the sentence does not refer to quantity or number, write ø.

1. I told the waiter that I would like to have _____ water.
2. _____ water is composed of hydrogen and oxygen.
3. I like Osaka. In fact, I have _____ friends there.
4. There are _____ pens on the table.
5. There is _____ apple juice in the refrigerator.
6. I talked to _____ friends after class.
7. Don't walk there! There's _____ broken glass on the floor.
8. The mailman put _____ letters in my mailbox.
9. I'm afraid I have _____ bad news.
10. _____ people need oxygen to live.

ANSWERS: 1. some, ø 2. ø 3. some, ø 4. some, ø 5. some, ø 6. some, ø 7. some, ø 8. some, ø 9. Some, ø 10. ø

NOTE: Numbers 2 and 10 cannot take *some* because they do not refer to an unspecified quantity or
number. <u>All</u> water is composed of hydrogen and oxygen—not just <u>some</u> water. <u>All</u> people need
oxygen to live—not just <u>some</u> people.

BEYOND THE RULES

Some and *any* are used only with indefinite noncount or indefinite plural nouns. Write *some* in the space if the sentence is positive and *any* if the sentence is negative.

1. I don't have _____ money.

2. There aren't _____ snakes in Ireland.

3. After the storm, there were _____ leaves in the street.

4. Put _____ butter in that pan, or the egg will start to stick.

ANSWERS: 1. any 2. any 3. some 4. some

✔ Quick Check

Check the INCORRECT sentences.

❏ 1. John didn't bring any pencil with him to the test.

❏ 2. Margaret doesn't have any car.

❏ 3. I sent Mary some flowers.

❏ 4. I don't have any plans for this evening.

❏ 5. I need some match.

ANSWERS: 1, 2 , 5 (Numbers 3 and 4 are correct.)

> NOTE: Numbers 1 and 2 are incorrect because *any* is not used for singular count nouns. Number 5 is incorrect because the sentence does not refer to an unspecified quantity or number.

Now write sentences 1, 2, and 5 correctly.

1. _____

2. _____

5. _____

ANSWERS: 1. John didn't bring a pencil with him to the test. *or* John didn't bring any pencils with him to the test. 2. Margaret doesn't have a car. *or* Margaret doesn't have any cars. 5. I need a match. *or* I need some matches.

You may use *any* or *some* in questions with indefinite plural or indefinite noncount nouns, but *any* is more common.

Write *some* or *any* in the spaces.

1. Do you have _____ money?

2. Did this patient have _____ food before the operation?

3. Is there _____ juice in the refrigerator?

4. Have you read _____ books by John Steinbeck?

ANSWERS: Either the word *any* or *some* is correct in 1 through 4.

Articles in Context

Read the following story carefully. Then read the questions and complete the answers. Read the story again to check your answers.

Seventeen Minutes Late

Lee arrived a little early for a quiz in a class. His teacher said, "You're early! Come back in thirteen minutes. Then, we'll begin the quiz."

3   Lee went to a cafe and drank a cup of coffee. He talked to some friends for ten minutes. Then the classmates left the cafe. Lee had another cup of coffee. He ordered bread and cheese. He didn't have enough time to finish the bread because it was getting late. Lee ran back to take
6   the quiz. When he got back, the teacher said, "You're late! The quiz is over. What happened? I thought I told you to come back in thirteen minutes."

"Oh," Lee answered. "I thought you said *thirty* minutes!"

What was Lee going to do?	He was going to take _____ quiz.
What did the teacher say?	She said that they would begin _____ quiz in thirteen minutes.
Where did Lee go?	He went to _____ cafe.
Did he talk to anyone?	He talked to _____ friends.
Who were they?	_____ friends were classmates.
What did they do?	They left _____ cafe.
What did Lee order?	He ordered _____ bread and cheese.
Did he eat all of it?	No, he didn't finish _____ bread.

Quiz 3

Write *the*, *a*, or *an* in the space provided. If no article is needed, write ø in the space. Then check your answers in the back of the book.

1. Amelia Earhart was flying a plane over the Pacific. _____ plane disappeared.

2. I don't particularly like _____ cream in tea or coffee.

3. John took Mary out to a movie. Mary didn't like _____ movie.

4. _____ honest politician is sometimes hard to find.

5. Clocks measure _____ time.

Rule 14: Use *the* when the noun that follows is already known.

NOTE: When the noun is understood or very obvious, it is already definite or "known."

> Be careful! You're spilling coffee on the floor.
> I picked up my suitcase and the handle broke off.
> Don't light that cigar! You'll fill the house with smoke.

EXERCISE C3

Write *the* in the space if the word is already known.

1. Marvin went fishing, stood up in the boat, and fell in _____ water.
2. I don't like traveling by air. I'm always afraid _____ plane will crash.
3. The teacher asked a question, but Mr. Jones didn't know _____ answer.
4. Kyoko can't study in Australia because she doesn't know _____ language.
5. Jim's mother said, "Jimmy, get your feet off _____ table!"

ANSWERS: 1. the 2. the 3. the 4. the 5. the

✔ Quick Check

Check the sentences in which the highlighted words have <u>not</u> been mentioned.

❑ 1. Masahiro swung the bat, hit a home run, and won the game.
❑ 2. An unusual animal lives in China. The animal is the panda.
❑ 3. Jason bought a house in 1985. He sold the house a year later.
❑ 4. Don't hit the window! You'll break the glass.
❑ 5. Could you answer the telephone please?

ANSWERS: 1, 4, and 5 These nouns take *the*, even though the nouns have not been mentioned, because they are very obvious. The others take *the* because they have already been mentioned.

PUTTING IT TOGETHER

Write *a*, *an* or *the* in the space. If no article is needed, write ø.

The Tell-Tale Boat Hitch

Jane went to buy _____ used car at Hal's Used
              1

Car Lot. She went to _____ lot in _____ afternoon
                      2   3

after work and immediately saw _____ car she liked.
                                4

_____ car was _____ old Ford. She kicked _____
5   6   7

tires (as all customers do when they buy _____ car).
                                          8

Then she got in _____ car and sat behind _____ wheel. When she looked at _____ odometer,
                9   10   11

she noticed that _____ car had 150,000 miles on it. "That's an awful lot of mileage," she
                 12

thought.

Just then _____ salesman came up to the window and said, "This car was owned by _____
          13   14

old lady. _____ lady taught grade school and only drove _____ car to work in _____ morning
          15   16   17

and home at _____ night."
            18

Jane got out and pointed to the back of the car. "What's that?" she asked.

"That," said _____ salesman, "is a hitch for pulling a boat."
             19

"Did _____ old lady always bring a boat to school?" Jane asked. Naturally, Jane decided
     20

not to buy the car.

ANSWERS: 1. a 2. the 3. the 4. a 5. the 6. an 7. the 8. a 9. the 10. the 11. the 12. the 13. a 14 an 15. the
16. the 17. the 18. ø 19. the 20. the

Comprehensive Test 2

Complete the sentences with the correct article. If no article is needed, write ø in the space. Then check your answers in the back of the book.

1. A snail moves only a few inches _____ hour.

2. A storm struck the coast of Sumatra. _____ storm caused a lot of damage.

3. A thousand is ten times more than _____ hundred.

4. _____ eulogy is usually a speech about someone who has died.

5. _____ unknown person stole a TV from Mr. Green's home.

6. I know the melody of that song, but I don't know _____ words.

7. I made some coffee. _____ coffee was too strong.

8. _____ "E" looks like a "3" in a mirror.

9. My friend went skiing and fell in _____ snow.

10. My last name begins with _____ C.

11. My uncle started a new company, but _____ company failed.

12. Nocturnal animals are animals that are active at _____ night.

13. Our guests have arrived. Will you answer _____ door?

14. That salesman is not _____ honest man.

15. The Chinese invented _____ gunpowder.

16. The space shuttle can travel at seven miles _____ second.

17. We bought a new car yesterday, and _____ car broke down today.

18. Yes, I know that book. _____ author is a friend of mine.

19. You made a key for me, but _____ key doesn't open the door.

20. Your plane leaves at 7:30 in _____ morning.

CHAPTER TWO

Read the rules for Part D and study the examples. Do not try to memorize the rules. Instead, do the exercises that follow the rules.

> **Rule 15: Use *the* when the noun is made definite by a prepositional phrase.**
>
> The back of this room is dirty.
> The prerequisites for this class are algebra and chemistry.
> The man in the red shirt is my boss.

EXERCISE D1

Write the correct article. Then write the correct preposition in the space.

of   in   on   at   to

1. _____ roof _____ my house needs repair.
2. The teacher erased _____ blackboard _____ our classroom.
3. _____ book _____ the table is mine.
4. _____ man _____ the door is a salesman.
5. Where is _____ key _____ this room?

ANSWERS: 1. the/of 2. the/in (or of) 3. The/on 4. The/at 5. the/to

> **Exception to Rule 15: Do not use *the* when the prepositional phrase does not make the noun definite.**
>
> I'd like a cup of soup.   (any cup, not a definite cup)
> Is there an eraser on your desk?   (any eraser, not a definite eraser)
> Do you need a pencil with an eraser?   (any pencil, not a definite pencil)

EXERCISE D2

Sentences 1-5 in Exercise D1 are definite because the prepositional phrase <u>identifies</u> the noun. The following exercise shows how a prepositional phrase can <u>identify</u> a noun and make it definite.

1. Look again at number 1 in Exercise D1.   Which roof needs repair?

_____*the roof of my house*_____

2. Look at number 2 in Exercise D1.   Which chalkboard did the teacher erase?

_____

3.   Look at number 3 in Exercise D1.   Which book is yours?

_____

4.   Look at number 4 in Exercise D1.   Which man is a salesman?

_____

5.   Look at number 5 in Exercise D1.   Which key are you looking for?

_____

ANSWERS: 2. the chalkboard in our classroom 3. the book on the table 4. the man at the door 5. the key to this room

The highlighted nouns in the following sentences are indefinite. The prepositional phrases are in **bold** type. Answer the questions by writing an "A" or a "B" in the space.

1.   There is a country **to the north of Malaysia.**

   Does the prepositional phrase tell you which country it is?   _____

        A. Yes, it identifies which country it is.

        B. No, it doesn't identify which country it is.

2.   Kristen said, "I'd like a piece **of paper**, please."

   Which piece does Kristen want?   _____

     A. She doesn't say. She wants any piece and doesn't care which.

     B. She identifies a specific piece that she wants.

3.   Jim Smith saw a man **in the park.**

   Do you know the identity of the man?   _____

     A. No. The sentence only tells where he is.

     B. Yes. I know exactly which man Jim saw.

ANSWERS: 1. B 2. A 3. A

PUTTING IT TOGETHER

Write *a*, *an*, or *the* in the spaces and answer the questions by writing an "A" or a "B" in the space.

1. _____ man **in the blue shirt** is Larry's friend.

    Which man is Larry's friend?   2. _____

    A. the man in the blue shirt

    B. The sentence doesn't identify which man is Larry's friend.

3. There is _____ eraser **on the desk.**

    Does the prepositional phrase tell which eraser is on the desk?   4. _____

    A. No. The sentence only tells where it is.

    B. Yes. It tells which eraser is on the desk.

5. Jan said, "I want to buy _____ computer **with a lot of memory."**

    Which computer does Jan want to buy?   6. _____

    A. She doesn't say. She wants to buy a computer with a lot of memory but
       she doesn't say which specific computer it is.

    B. She knows exactly which computer she wants to buy.

7. _____ air **in this city** is dirty.

    Which air is dirty?   8. _____

    A. The sentence doesn't identify which air.

    B. the air in this city

ANSWERS: 1. The 2. A 3. an 4. A 5. a 6. A 7. The 8. B

EXERCISE D3

Write the correct article in the space. If the word is not made definite by the highlighted prepositional phrase, do not write *the*; write *a*, *an*, or *ø* instead.

1. Mr. Jones was hungry, so he ate _____ piece of cake.
2. Sally has _____ piano in her house.
3. I ordered _____ coffee with cream.
4. Waiter! There's _____ fly in my soup!
5. _____ water in Lake Itasca is clean.

Answers: 1. a 2. a 3. ø 4. a 5. The

> NOTE: Only in number 5 is the word made definite by the prepositional phrase.

✔ Quick Check

Check the INCORRECT sentences.

❑ 1. Look out! There's the spider on your shoulder!
❑ 2. Who is a president of that company?
❑ 3. Do you know an answer to question number 5?
❑ 4. I want to buy a car with a CD player.
❑ 5. He was born on a day before Christmas.

ANSWERS: 1, 2, 3, 5 (Number 4 is correct.)

Now, write the INCORRECT sentences correctly.

1. _____
2. _____
3. _____
4. *I want to buy a car with a CD player.*_____
5. _____

In which of the five sentences above does the prepositional phrase NOT make the noun definite?

ANSWERS: 1 and 4 (All of the others take *the*.)

ANSWERS: 1. Look out! There's a spider on your shoulder! 2. Who is the president of that company? 3. Do you know the answer to question number 5? 5. He was born on the day before Christmas.

PUTTING IT TOGETHER

Write the correct article in the space. Do not write *the* if the prepositional phrase does NOT make the word definite; write *a*, *an*, or ø instead.

1. Daley Park was almost empty. I saw only _____ man with a dog.
2. I'm so absent-minded! I just locked _____ keys to my car inside the car.
3. _____ day after tomorrow is Saturday.
4. There's _____ law against drinking and driving.
5. Is there _____ FAX machine in your office?
6. _____ umbrella near the door is mine.
7. I don't know _____ answer to question number 7.
8. I want you to clean _____ top of the refrigerator.
9. Jim just bought _____ pack of cigarettes.
10. Do you have _____ radio in your car?

ANSWERS: 1. a 2. the 3. The 4. a 5. a 6. The 7. the 8. the 9. a 10. a

BEYOND THE RULES

In Rule 14, you learned that some words are definite because they are already known, very obvious, or understood. You can often imagine prepositional phrases that go with such words.

Write *the* and a prepositional phrase to go with the highlighted words.

> You see: I picked up my suitcase and the handle broke.
> You write: The handle of my suitcase broke.

1. Ana got in her car and sat behind the wheel.

    Ana sat behind _____ wheel _____.

2. I went to England and met the Queen.

    I met _____ Queen _____.

3. That book was popular and the author got rich.

    _____ author _____ got rich.

4. I can't open this door. Do you have the key?

    Do you have _____ key _____?

5. I was uncomfortable at Margaret's party because I didn't know the people.

    I didn't know _____ people _____.

6. The sign in the park said: "Don't walk on the grass!"

    Don't walk on _____ grass _____!

7. I was driving my car when suddenly the engine stalled.

    _____ engine _____ stalled.

8. The doctors at Mercy Hospital give the patients excellent care.

    _____ patients _____ receive excellent care.

9. I can't answer your question because I don't know the answer.

    I don't know _____ answer _____.

10. I enjoy traveling in Mexico because I speak the language.

    _____ language _____ is Spanish.

ANSWERS: 1. the wheel of her car 2. the Queen of England 3. The author of that book 4. the key to this door
5. the people at Margaret's party 6. the grass in the park 7. The engine of my car 8. The patients at
Mercy Hospital 9. the answer to your question 10. The language of (or in) Mexico

BEYOND THE RULES

Prepositional phrases with *of* often make a word definite, so *the* is used. However, *of* and *the* also go together in other ways. In the following exercises, *of the* is used to show that the word is special or definite. *Of the* is not used to <u>generalize</u> about the word.

Most	All	Some	Many	Much
Most of the	All of the	Some of the	Many of the	Much of the

INDEFINITE: Most people like to laugh. (a generalization about people)

DEFINITE: Most of the people in my class like to laugh. (specific people)

Write *most of the* if a prepositional phrase makes the underlined word definite. If not, write *most*.

1. _____ cats won't drink coconut milk.
2. _____ buildings near the center of town were damaged.
3. _____ people at the party enjoyed themselves.
4. _____ people don't like snakes.
5. Albert has read _____ books on that shelf.

ANSWERS: 1. Most 2. Most of the 3. Most of the 4. Most 5. most of the

Write *all of the* if a prepositional phrase makes the underlined word definite. If not, write *all*.

1. I don't know _____ people in my hometown.
2. Not _____ fish lay eggs.
3. _____ words on the chalkboard were misspelled.
4. Almost _____ cars have seat belts today.
5. Almost _____ people in North Dakota speak English.

ANSWERS: 1. all of the 2. all 3. All of the 4. all 5. all of the

Write *of the* if a prepositional phrase makes the underlined word definite. If not, write ø.

1. Some _____ birds cannot fly.
2. Many _____ people like spicy food.
3. Most _____ water on the earth is salty.
4. Much _____ wine from France is sold abroad.
5. Many _____ houses near the airport are inexpensive.

ANSWERS: 1. ø 2. ø 3. of the 4. of the

PUTTING IT TOGETHER

Write the correct article in each space.

Silver Springs is _____ small mining town south of Bell Mountain. In _____ southern part of
                        1   2
_____ town, there is _____ residential area with about 300 people. Beyond _____ residential
  3   4   5
area is _____ large silver mine. Most of _____ people of Silver Springs work there. In _____
              6   7   8
middle of _____ town stands _____ tremendous smokestack. It is almost 700 feet in height.
                    9   10
_____ theater, _____ supermarket, and _____ shopping center can be seen on _____ western
  11   12   13   14
side of _____ town. At _____ northern end of Silver Springs, Bell Mountain is located. Beyond
              15   16
_____ mountain is _____ vast, empty desert. That's almost _____ complete description of _____
  17   18   19   20
town of Silver Springs. There are few towns as small.

ANSWERS: 1. a 2. the 3. the 4. a 5. the 6. a 7. the 8. the 9. the 10. a 11. a * 12. a * 13 a * 14. the 15. the
16. the 17. the 18. a 19. a 20. the

NOTE: If the theater, supermarket, and shopping center are already understood or known to the writer, the
article *the* may be used in 11, 12, and 13.

23

Write the correct article in each space. If no article is needed, write ø in the space. Then check your answers in the back of the book.

1. Is there _____ lake near your house?

2. _____ big tree next to my house is an elm.

3. I'd like _____ slice of bread.

4. _____ woman in the blue blouse is Mrs. Blake.

5. Who was the first person to climb to _____ top of Mount Everest?

Comprehensive Test 3

Write an article in each space. If no article is needed, write ø in the space. Then check your answers in the back of the book.

1. _____ oxygen has eight protons.

2. I read _____ book on geology last week.

3. _____ members of that band are very talented.

4. A birthday cake usually has _____ candles on it.

5. Many of _____ airliners in the world are made in Washington State.

6. Most _____ dogs hate cats.

7. All of _____ fish in that river died.

8. I picked up the sugar bowl, and some of _____ sugar fell on the floor.

9. Some _____ movies are good, and others aren't.

10. Is this _____ road to Santa Fe?

11. _____ pound of butter costs over two dollars in that store.

12. _____ area of a circle can be determined by the formula $A = \pi r^2$.

13. I usually have _____ glass of orange juice for breakfast.

14. There's _____ eucalyptus tree in my front yard.

15. _____ hydrogen is an explosive gas.

16. The Hayden Mill produces flour. _____ flour is sold locally.

17. I took some plums from the refrigerator. _____ plums were sweet and cold.

18. You can get that magazine for only fifty cents _____ issue.

19. I have an acoustic guitar. _____ strings are metal.

20. *Indonesia* begins with _____ "I."

Read the following rules and study the examples.

Rule 16: Use *the* when the noun is made definite by an adjective clause or an adjective phrase.

Adjective Clauses:

The teacher that we had last semester was especially good.
The man that hired me yesterday left the company today.
The car which the Smiths bought gets 50 miles a gallon.
The town where I grew up is now a big city.
The man she married was poor.

Adjective Phrases:

The woman standing by the door is my sister.
The teenagers living next door play loud music late at night.
The man arrested by the police went to jail.
The house destroyed by the fire was mine.

EXERCISE D4

Write *the* and the most logical adjective clause in each space.

that bit me	that we had for English class
that I live in	that she failed
who robbed the bank	that burned the forest

1. The police arrested _____ man _____.
2. _____ dog _____ ran away.
3. _____ teacher _____ was very good.
4. _____ house _____ is on Colt Road.
5. Jill has to repeat _____ classes _____.
6. Who started _____ fire _____?

ANSWERS: 1. the man who robbed the bank 2. The dog that bit me 3. the teacher that we had for English class
4. The house that I live in 5. the classes that she failed 6. the fire that burned the forest

Exception to Rule 16: Don't use *the* when the adjective clause or adjective phrase does not make the noun definite.

> I want a pen that works. (any pen that works)
> Yesterday night, I saw a man running down the street. (The man is not known.)

EXERCISE D5

Sentences 1-5 in Exercise D4 are definite because the adjective clause *identifies* the noun. The following exercise shows how an adjective clause can <u>identify</u> a noun and make it definite.

1. Look at number 1 in Exercise D4. Which man was arrested?

   _____

2. Look at number 2 in Exercise D4. Which dog ran away?

   _____

3. Look at number 3 in Exercise D4. Which teacher was good?

   _____

ANSWERS: 2. the dog that bit me 3. the teacher that we had for English class

The highlighted nouns in the following sentences are indefinite. Answer the questions by writing an A or a B in the space. Adjective clauses and adjective phrases are in **bold** type.

1. There is a large country **which lies to the south of the US.**

   Does the adjective clause tell you which country it is?   _____

       A. Yes, it identifies which country it is.

       B. No, it doesn't identify which country it is.

2. John said, "I'd like a pen **that writes**, please."

   Which pen does John want?   _____

       A. He doesn't say. He wants any pen that writes and doesn't care which.

       B. He identifies a specific pen that he wants.

3. Jim Smith saw a man **running in the park.**

   Do you know the identity of the man?   _____

       A. No. The sentence only tells what the man was doing.

       B. Yes. I know exactly which man Jim saw.

ANSWERS: 1. B 2. A 3. A

PUTTING IT TOGETHER

Write *a*, *an*, or *the* in the spaces. Then answer the questions by writing an A or a B in the space.

1. _____ man **standing by the door** is Larry's friend.

   Which man is Larry's friend?   2. _____

      A. the man standing by the door

      B. The sentence doesn't identify which man is Larry's friend.

3. There is _____ eraser **lying on the desk.**

   Does the adjective phrase tell which eraser is on the desk?   4. _____

      A. No. The adjective phrase only tells where it is.

      B. Yes. It tells which eraser is lying on the desk.

5. Jan said, "I want to buy _____ computer that has a lot of memory."

   Which computer does Jan want to buy?   6. _____

      A. She doesn't say. She wants to buy a computer that has a lot of memory, but she
         doesn't say which specific computer it is.

      B. She knows exactly which computer she wants to buy.

7. _____ air that people have to breathe in this city is dirty.

   Which air is dirty?   8. _____

      A. The sentence doesn't identify which air.

      B. the air that people have to breathe in this city

ANSWERS: 1. The 2. A 3. an 4. A 5. a 6. A 7. The 8. B

EXERCISE D6

Write the correct article in the space. If the word is NOT made definite by the highlighted adjective clause, do not write *the*; write *a*, *an*, or *ø* instead.

1. I need _____ computer that has a hard drive.
2. _____ woman who wrote *Gone with the Wind* died tragically.
3. At school, there are ___ computers the students and teachers can use.
4. My boss is looking for _____ assistant who can help him with computers.
5. I'd like to buy _____ car that has an air bag.

ANSWERS: 1. a 2. The 3. ø 4. an 5. a

> NOTE: Only in number 2 is the word made definite by the adjective clause. Remember Rule 6: Nouns after *there* + "be" are never definite (See number 3 above).

✓ Quick Check

Check the INCORRECT sentences. Adjective clauses and important articles are highlighted.

❑ 1. A town where I was born is in the Midwest.
❑ 2. A girl who is wearing the red skirt is my sister.
❑ 3. Apples which we ate were delicious.
❑ 4. Do you remember the name of a woman who called?
❑ 5. O. Henry often wrote stories that had surprise endings.

ANSWERS: 1, 2, 3, 4 (Number 5 is correct).

Now, write the INCORRECT sentences correctly.

1. _____
2. _____
3. _____
4. _____

In which of the five sentences above does the adjective clause NOT make the word definite? _____

ANSWER: 5. (All of the others take *the* because they identify the noun.)

ANSWERS: 1. The town where I was born is in the Midwest. 2. The girl who is wearing the red skirt is my sister. 3. The apples which we ate were delicious. 4. Do you remember the name of the woman who called?

EXERCISE D7

Write *the* and the logical adjective phrase in the spaces.

cooking on the stove	stolen from the parking lot
invited to her party	growing in my garden
written for this class	flying that noisy plane

1. _____ car _____ was mine.
2. Who is _____ pilot _____ up there?
3. Mary is sad; none of _____ people _____ came.
4. _____ papers _____ must be typed.
5. _____ flowers _____ are beautiful.
6. _____ soup _____ is not ready yet.

ANSWERS: 1. The car stolen from the parking lot 2. the pilot flying that noisy plane 3. the people invited to her party 4. The papers written for this class 5. The flowers growing in my garden 6. The soup cooking on the stove

EXERCISE D8

Now change the phrases in these sentences to clauses by writing *the*, *that*, and the correct form of the verb "be."

You see: _____ car _____ stolen from the parking lot was mine.

You write: *The* car ___*that was*___ stolen from the parking lot was mine.

1. Who is _____ pilot _____ flying that noisy plane up there?
2. Mary is sad; none of _____ people _____ invited to her party came.
3. _____ papers _____ written for this class must be typed.
4. _____ flowers _____ growing in my garden are beautiful.
5. _____ soup _____ cooking on the stove is not ready yet.

ANSWERS: 1. the pilot that is 2. the people that were 3. The papers that are (or that will be) 4. The flowers that are 5. The soup that is

BEYOND THE RULES

In Rule 13, you learned that some words are definite because they have already been mentioned. You can often imagine adjective clauses that go with such words.

Write *the* and an adjective clause to go with the highlighted words. Use *that* in each answer.

> You see: I saw a dog. The dog bit me.
> You write: __*The*__ dog __*that I saw*__ bit me.

1. Jack built a house. The house burned down last year.

   _____ house _____ burned down last year.

2. Dr. Castle treated a patient. The patient got well.

   _____ patient _____ got well.

3. I planted a garden. The garden grew.

   _____ garden _____ grew.

4. Mr. Burroughs wrote a book. The book was **Tarzan of the Apes**.

   _____ book _____ was **Tarzan of the Apes**.

5. Frogs live in that lake. The frogs are noisy.

   _____ frogs _____ are noisy.

6. I saw some planes. The planes landed in a field.

   _____ planes _____ landed in a field.

7. A man came to the door. The man was a salesman.

   _____ man _____ was a salesman.

8. Lightning struck the mountain. The lightning started a fire.

   _____ lightning _____ started a fire.

9. The Browns adopted three children. The children were refugees.

   _____ children _____ were refugees.

10. Snow fell on that mountain in July. The snow quickly melted.

    _____ snow _____ quickly melted.

ANSWERS: 1. The house that Jack built 2. The patient that Dr. Castle treated 3. The garden that I planted 4. The book that Mr. Burroughs wrote 5. The frogs that live in that lake 6. The planes that I saw 7. The man that came to the door 8. The lightning that struck the mountain 9. The children that the Browns adopted 10. The snow that fell on that mountain in July

BEYOND THE RULES

Write *of the* if an adjective clause or adjective phrase makes the highlighted words definite. If not, write ø.

1. Many _____ trees burned in the forest fire were very old.
2. Most _____ Americans speak English.
3. Jan spent all _____ money she earned in the summer.
4. Almost all _____ students who attended the class passed.
5. Many _____ people graduating today are over fifty years old.
6. Some _____ papers we were carrying fell on the floor.
7. Most _____ Koreans that I know are from Seoul.
8. Some _____ people cannot sing very well.
9. The Salt River supplies much _____ water used in my hometown.
10. Many _____ children love dinosaurs.

ANSWERS: 1. of the 2. ø 3. of the 4. of the 5. of the 6. of the 7. of the 8. ø 9. of the 10. ø

Write *of the* if the word has already been mentioned or if it is already known. If not, write ø.

1. Most of the boys in my school play baseball, and most _____ girls don't.
2. There are twenty kids in Mr. Kim's class. All _____ kids like his class.
3. Many _____ snakes lay eggs, and all _____ birds do.
4. I gave the young child a book, but she tore out all _____ pages.
5. That's an old neighborhood, and some _____ houses need repair.

ANSWERS: 1. of the 2. of the 3. ø, ø 4. of the 5. of the

ARTICLES IN CONTEXT

Read the following story carefully and complete the answers to the questions. Then read the story again to check your work.

The Office Visitor

   A poorly-dressed man entered an office in the University of Littletown. The man's
3 hair was long and stringy, and the coat that he was wearing was old and dirty. "Excuse me," he said apologetically. "I think I am
6 lost."

   The secretary who was sitting at the desk in the office looked up at him and frowned.
9 "I <u>know</u> you are," she said coldly and looked down at the papers lying on her desk.

   "I can't find the person whom I came to
12 see," the man said. "He's expecting me."

   "Well, the person expecting you is certainly not here," said the secretary impolitely. "Good day, sir."

15 "Will you at least tell me where the Department of Chemistry is?" asked the man. "I drove all the way from Bigcity."

   This is the Chemistry Department," answered the secretary, "—but did you say Bigcity? Are
18 you . . .?"

   "I am Dr. James Crawford," the man replied.

   The frown on the secretary's face disappeared and she smiled sweetly. "Oh, what a pleasure
21 it is to meet you, Professor Crawford. Welcome! Welcome to Littletown!"

Who entered the office?	_____ poorly-dressed man.
What did his coat look like?	_____ coat he was wearing was old and dirty.
Whom did he talk to?	_____ secretary who was sitting there.
What was the man's problem?	He couldn't find _____ person that he came to see.
What department was he looking for?	_____ Department of Chemistry.
What disappeared?	_____ frown on the secretary's face.
Who was the secretary's boss?	Probably _____ person expecting Dr. Crawford.

 **Quiz 5**

Write the correct article in the space provided. If no article is needed, write ø in the space. Then check your answers in the back of the book.

1. _____ woman that Mozart married was a poor housekeeper.
2. There's _____ movie that I want to see on TV.
3. Almost all of _____ people in my family live in the same city.
4. _____ guitar that I bought for forty dollars in 1960 is now worth more than one thousand.
5. There's _____ bunch of grapes in the refrigerator.

> **Rule 17: Do not use an article with the names of streets, avenues, roads, lanes, or boulevards.**
>
> Correct: I live on Ninth Street.
> Correct: Broadway is a famous street in New York City.
> Correct: That store is located on Eighth Avenue.
> Correct: Recker Road is busy during rush hour.
> Correct: Cherry Lane runs parallel to Colt Road.
> Correct: Harris Boulevard crosses Main Street.
>
> Incorrect: I live on the Ninth Street.
> Incorrect: A Broadway is a famous street in New York City.

EXERCISE D9

Write the correct article in the space. If no article is needed, write ø.

1. Cross _____ Thirtieth Avenue and turn right on _____ Elm.
2. Mr. West lived on _____ Sierra Vista Lane for almost thirty years.
3. I can't remember the name of _____ street that she lives on.
4. There's _____ road in front of my house.
5. Do _____ Paine Avenue and _____ 34th Street run parallel to each other?

ANSWERS: 1. ø, ø 2. ø 3. the 4. a 5. ø, ø

NOTE: Numbers 3 and 4 do not contain the names of streets or roads.

EXERCISE D10

Study the map. Then complete the sentences by writing the correct street names.

```
                              N
        _____            |    _____
                            |
          Fifth      ≡      |      Street
        _____      M     |    _____
                      i     |
   W                  l     |              E
        _____      l     |    _____
                      A     |
         Apache       v     |     Boulevard
        _____      e     |    _____
                      n     |
                      u     |
                      e     |
                              S
```

1. Mill Avenue crosses _____ and _____ .
2. Apache Boulevard crosses _____ .
3. _____ runs north and south.
4. _____ runs parallel to _____ .
5. _____ and _____ run east and west.

ANSWERS: 1. Apache Boulevard/Fifth Street (or the reverse) 2. Mill Avenue 3. Mill Avenue 4. Apache Boulevard/Fifth Street (or the reverse) 5. Apache Boulevard/Fifth Street (or the reverse)

BEYOND THE RULES

Street names are often used as adjectives in English.

Write the correct article (*the*, *a*, or *an*) in each space. Note that the name of a street is used as an adjective in each sentence.

1. _____ Broadway play that we saw was excellent.
2. _____ A Madison Avenue lawyer can charge 300 dollars an hour.
3. We stopped in New Orleans to hear _____ Bourbon Street jazz band.
4. Mr. Jones is the owner of _____ Central Avenue restaurant where I work.

ANSWERS: 1. The 2. A 3. a 4. the

Rule 18: Do not use an article when generalizing about abstract nouns.

Correct: Love is a beautiful thing.
Correct: Peace is something all people want.
Correct: Crime is a growing problem.
Correct: Everyone is worried about inflation.

Incorrect: The love is a beautiful thing.
Incorrect: A peace is something all citizens want.

Abstract nouns are nouns that you cannot see, touch, or feel. As noncount nouns they do not take *a* or *an*. (Rule 4)

NOTE: While it is possible to "feel" love, hate, or friendship, it is not possible to feel these things in the physical way that you can feel air, salt, or wind. Love, hate, and friendship are abstract nouns.

✔ Quick Check

All of the following words are noncount nouns. Check the abstract nouns (the ones that you cannot see, touch, or feel).

❏	1.	sand	❏	6.	strength	❏	11.	cotton
❏	2.	employment	❏	7.	cheese	❏	12	goodness
❏	3.	water	❏	8.	advice	❏	13.	gold
❏	4.	protection	❏	9.	food	❏	14.	learning
❏	5.	fuel	❏	10.	weight	❏	15.	money

ANSWER: The even numbers (2, 4, 6, 8, etc.) are abstract nouns. The odd numbers (1, 3, 5, 7, etc.) are not.

EXERCISE D11

Write ø if the sentence <u>generalizes</u> about the highlighted abstract noun. If not, write *the*.

1. _____ beauty is only skin deep.
2. _____ faith and _____ patience are wonderful qualities.
3. _____ love that he had for her was deep.
4. That man is only interested in _____ wealth.
5. _____ friendship that we shared was important to me.

ANSWERS: 1. ø 2. ø 3. The 4. ø 5. The

NOTE: Sentences 3 and 5 do not generalize about the abstract noun because adjective clauses make the nouns definite.

✔ Quick Check

Many abstract nouns can also be count nouns. Write *a* or *ø* in the spaces. Then check the sentences that have count nouns.

❑ 1. For centuries _____ war has plagued mankind.
❑ 2. The people in that country were the victims of ___ short but tragic war.
❑ 3. People learn quickly by _____ experience.
❑ 4. I had _____ wonderful experience working in Yellowstone Park.
❑ 5. _____ violent crime is committed most often at night.
❑ 6. The man committed _____ terrible crime and had to go to prison.

ANSWERS: 1. ø 2. a 3. ø 4. a 5. ø 6. a Check sentences 2, 4, and 6.

Count nouns have plural forms. Rewrite sentences 2, 4, and 6 using the plural form of the highlighted word.

_____

_____

_____

ANSWERS: 2. The people in that country were the victims of short but tragic wars. 4. I had wonderful experiences working in Yellowstone Park. 6. The man committed terrible crimes and had to go to prison.

BEYOND THE RULES

Abstract nouns often have adjective forms. Here are just a few examples.

Adjectives	Abstract Nouns
happy	happiness
honest	honesty
patient	patience
wise	wisdom

From the list above, choose the most logical abstract noun for each space. Write *the* with the abstract noun if the noun is definite.

1. That man always lies. _____ means nothing to him.
2. The opposite of sadness is _____.
3. Don't be in such a hurry. Have _____!
4. Old people are often wise. You should respect _____ of an older person.

ANSWERS: 1. Honesty 2. happiness 3. patience 4. the wisdom

NOTE: Number 4 takes *the* because the noun is made definite by a prepositional phrase.

36

Adjectives	Abstract Nouns
deep	depth
high	height
long	length
wide	width

From the list above, choose the most logical abstract noun. Write *the* with the abstract noun if the noun is definite.

1. The Amazon River is almost 4000 miles in _____.
2. Sonar can determine _____ of a lake or ocean.
3. What is _____ of Mount Fuji?
4. Office paper is 8 1/2 inches in _____.

ANSWERS: 1. length 2. the depth 3. the height 4. width Note: Numbers 2 and 3 take *the* because the nouns are made definite by prepositional phrases.

Abstract nouns also often have verbal forms. Here are just a few examples:

Verbs	Abstract Nouns
advise	advice
cry	crying
protect	protection
know	knowledge
weigh	weight

From the list above, choose the most logical abstract noun. Write *the* with the abstract noun if the noun is definite.

1. Ignorance can be defined as the lack of _____.
2. The new foreign student adviser gave me some excellent _____.
3. You look so thin! Have you lost _____?
4. _____ that a seatbelt provides is substantial.
5. Laughing is better than _____.

ANSWERS: 1. knowledge 2. advice 3. weight 4. The protection 5. crying

NOTE: Number 4 takes *the* because the noun is made definite by an adjective clause.

PUTTING IT TOGETHER

Write the correct article in each space. If no article is needed, write ø.

1. _____ love and _____ hate are opposites.
2. _____ courage that she showed was remarkable.
3. _____ punishment for robbery is imprisonment.
4. People should not be punished for _____ beliefs that they hold.
5. The Pyramid of the Sun in Mexico is made of _____ stone.
6. We're having _____ wonderful time and wish that you were here.

ANSWERS: 1. ø 2. The 3. The 4. the 5. ø 6. a

NOTE: Of the above underlined words, only *stone* is not an abstract noun.

Articles in Context

Read the following story carefully and answer the questions with *the*, *a*, *an*, or *ø*. Then read the story again to check your answers.

The Fisherman's Secret

Jim and Brent went fishing one summer morning. They started fishing at six o'clock.
3 At 6:10, Brent said, "Let me tell you a little fisherman's secret. Do you want to catch some fish?"

6   "Of course I do," replied Jim. "What's the secret?"

       "FAITH AND PATIENCE!" shouted
9 Brent loudly. "PATIENCE AND FAITH! That's all you need to catch fish!"

       "Shh!" whispered Jim. "Faith and
12 patience are fine, but you also need <u>silence</u>. You'll scare the fish."

       At 6:20, Brent whispered to Jim, "Faith and patience!"

15   At 6:30, he looked at Jim and asked, "Have you got a bite yet?" Jim answered, "Not yet."

       At 6:35, Brent said, "I'm going home!"

       "Home?" Jim responded. "We just got here. Why do you want to leave?"

18   "Because I don't think we're going to catch any fish," Brent said angrily. "Besides, I'm tired of waiting around!"

What did Brent tell Jim?	_____ little fisherman's secret
What was the secret?	_____ faith and _____ patience
Why did Jim say "Shh!"?	He was afraid Brent would scare _____ fish.
What did Jim want?	He wanted _____ silence.
Why did Brent want to go home?	He didn't have _____ faith or _____ patience.

38

Read the following rule and study the examples.

> **Rule 19: Do not use an article when generalizing in the plural.**
>
> Correct: Cats can climb trees but dogs can't. (all cats/all dogs)
> Correct: Palm trees are tropical plants. (all palm trees)
> Correct: Cars and trucks are useful machines. (all cars and trucks)
> Correct: People everywhere love music. (all people)
>
> Incorrect: The cats can climb trees but the dogs can't.
> Incorrect: The palm trees are common in tropical areas.
> Incorrect: The cars and the trucks are useful machines.
> Incorrect: The people everywhere love music.

When you generalize about a noun, it is indefinite, so *the* cannot be used (Rule 5), and plural nouns never take *a* or *an* (Rule 3).

EXERCISE D12

Write ø if the sentence <u>generalizes</u> about the highlighted plural noun. If not, write *the*.

1. _____ pigeons can find their way home from hundreds of miles away.
2. _____ pigeons that we feed at the park are not afraid of people.
3. I don't know anything about _____ cars.
4. I don't know anything about _____ cars produced in Britain.
5. _____ airplanes are fascinating machines.
6. _____ airplanes of World War II were fascinating machines.

ANSWERS: 1. ø 2. The 3. ø 4. the 5. ø 6. The

EXERCISE D13

Write *all* if the sentence generalizes about the highlighted plural noun. Write *all of the* if it doesn't.

1. _____ plants need sunshine.
2. _____ plants in my garden need sunshine.
3. Not _____ countries have an ocean.
4. Not _____ countries in Europe have an ocean.

ANSWERS: 1. All 2. All of the 3. all 4. all of the

Quiz 6

Write the correct article in the space provided. If no article is needed, write ø in the space. Then check your answers in the back of the book.

1. _____ Ocean Street runs north and south.
2. _____ greatness of a nation is measured by the work of its people.
3. _____ chimpanzees are the closest relatives of human beings.
4. I like seafood, especially _____ oysters.
5. "_____ cleanliness is next to godliness."

Comprehensive Test 4

Write an article in the space provided. If no article is needed, write ø in the space. Then check your answers in the back of the book.

1. In _____ town where I was born lived a man who sailed to sea.

2. _____ blue whales are the largest animals that ever lived.

3. You don't pronounce _____ "S" at the end of *Arkansas* or *Illinois*.

4. I spent the day at the ocean sitting on _____ shore.

5. Our store is on the northwest corner of _____ Main Street and Elm Road.

6. I saw _____ exciting soccer game last week.

7. She looked down at _____ papers lying on her desk.

8. I prefer apples to _____ oranges.

9. They're tearing up _____ street in front of my house.

10. _____ unemployment is a growing problem.

11. I don't have _____ house in the country.

12. Who is _____ person at the door?

13. When I have watermelon, I try not to eat _____ seeds.

14. I dropped a glass and _____ glass broke.

15. You cannot buy _____ happiness.

16. I'm glad that you had such _____ wonderful experiences here.

17. _____ gold used to cost only 35 dollars an ounce.

18. If you join the army, you will have to wear _____ uniform.

19. Do you know where _____ Cottage Lane is?

20. Almost all of _____ words he wrote were misspelled.

CHAPTER THREE

Part E

Read the rules for Part E and study the examples. Do not try to memorize the rules. Instead, do the exercises that follow the rules.

Rule 20: **Do not use an article with the names of universities or colleges.**

> Correct: He goes to Nanzan University in Japan.
> Correct: My professor graduated from Middlebury College.
>
> Incorrect: He goes to the Nanzan University in Japan.

Exception to Rule 20: **Use *the* with names of colleges and universities that contain the word *of*.**

> She attends the University of Salamanca in Spain.
> The College of Architecture is located in a beautiful building.

EXERCISE E1

Write *the* if the name of the university or college contains the word *of*. If not, write ø.

1. I work at a biology station for _____ University of Minnesota.
2. _____ Utah State University and _____ University of Utah are different schools.
3. _____ Kansai Gaidai University is in Japan.
4. _____ Colby College is located in Waterville, Maine.
5. Professor Powers works in _____ College of Engineering.

ANSWERS: 1. the 2. ø, the 3. ø 4. ø 5. the

PUTTING IT TOGETHER

Write the correct article in the space. If no article is needed, write ø.

1. _____ Oberlin College is in the state of Ohio.
2. _____ U of C is in San Diego, California.
3. I enrolled in _____ College of Fine Arts.
4. _____ Temasek Junior College is one of several junior colleges in Singapore.
5. There isn't _____ university in the town of Silver Springs.
6. _____ Harvard University degree is respected everywhere.

ANSWERS: 1. ø 2. The 3. the 4. ø 5. a 6. a

> NOTE: Number 5 does not contain the name of a university. In number 6, the <u>name</u> of the university is used as an adjective.

Rule 21: Do not use an article with the names of countries, cities, or states.

Correct: Germany borders France.
Correct: Peking is now usually called Beijing.
Correct: Minnesota has ten thousand lakes.

Incorrect: The Peking is now usually called the Beijing.

EXERCISE E2

Write the correct article in the space. If no article is needed, write ø.

1. The capital of _____ Thailand is Bangkok.
2. _____ Alabama is a southern state in the US.
3. Puerto Peñasco is a city in _____ Mexico.
4. _____ Chicago is called "the Windy City."
5. _____ Australia is an island continent.
6. There's a song about _____ Kansas City, Missouri.

ANSWERS: 1. ø 2. ø 3. ø 4. ø 5. ø 6. ø

Exception to Rule 21: Use *the* in the names of countries that contain the words *united, union, kingdom,* or *republic.*

The United Arab Emirates is a country in the Middle East.
Riyadh is the capital of the Kingdom of Saudi Arabia.
The Republic of South Africa occupies over 471,000 square miles.

EXERCISE E3

Write *the* if the name of the country contains the word *united, union, kingdom,* or *republic.* Otherwise, write ø.

1. _____ Scotland is a part of _____ United Kingdom.
2. How long have you been in _____ United States?
3. Where is _____ People's Republic of China?
4. _____ Canada is the second largest country in the world.
5. _____ Kingdom of Morroco is south of Spain.

ANSWERS: 1. ø, the 2. the 3. the 4. ø 5. The

BEYOND THE RULES

Abbreviations with letters for the names of countries which contain the word *united*, *union*, or *kingdom* also take *the*.

Write the correct article in the space.

1. _____ Union of Soviet Socialist Republics no longer exists.
2. _____ USSR no longer exists.
3. _____ United Kingdom is also called _____ UK.
4. _____ United Arab Emirates is a small country.
5. _____ UAE is a small country.
6. My car was made in _____ USA.

ANSWERS: 1. The 2. The 3. The, the 4. The 5. The 6. the

PUTTING IT TOGETHER

Write the correct article in the space. If no article is needed, write ø.

Helga's Dilemma

Helga Schmidt has _____ decision to make. She is _____ German student, and
              1   2
two universities have accepted her into their colleges of music: _____ University of
                                                                  3
Littletown in _____ US and _____ Cambridge University in England. Helga has always
              4   5
wanted to visit _____ America, and she has already been to _____ Britain many times.
                6   7
However, her brother lives in _____ England, and she can stay with him and save money
                              8
on rent. She also has _____ sister who goes to _____ Cambridge University. Helga
                      9   10
knows that _____ Littletown is _____ famous city for music, but Helga doesn't think that
           11   12
_____ U of L is as prestigious _____ school as _____ Cambridge University. She can't
13   14   15
decide whether she should go to _____ US or _____ UK.
                                16   17

ANSWERS: 1. a 2. a 3. the 4. ø 5. ø 6. ø 7. ø 8. ø 9. a 10. ø 11. ø 12. a 13. the 14. a 15. ø 16. the 17. the

BEYOND THE RULES

The names of cities, states, and countries are proper nouns and can be definite without the word *the*. Many other proper nouns work the same way.

The highlighted noun in each of the following sentences is definite. Write ø in the space before the proper nouns. Otherwise write *the*.

1. _____ country where my English teacher was born has fifty states.
2. _____ Canada, where my English teacher was born, has ten provinces.
3. _____ Seoul, South Korea, where Lee grew up, has a cold winter.
4. _____ city where Lee grew up has a cold winter.
5. _____ country that I visit every summer has many mountains.
6. _____ Japan, which I visit every summer, has many mountains.
7. _____ girl who got the highest grades received a scholarship.
8. _____ Mary, who got the highest grades, received a scholarship.
9. _____ man who wrote "The Black Cat" died at the age of 42.
10. _____ Edgar Allan Poe, who wrote "The Black Cat," died at the age of 42.

ANSWERS: 1. The 2. ø 3. ø 4. The 5. The 6. ø 7. The 8. ø 9. The 10. ø

BEYOND THE RULES

Possessive Adjectives (*my, your, his her*, etc.) indicate a definite noun. They can take the place of *the* in some sentences.

Write the most logical possessive adjective in the space. Then, write *the* in the same sentence.

               my   your   her

1. Sue has a brother and a sister. I've met _____ brother but not _____ sister.
1. Sue has a brother and a sister. I've met _____ brother but not _____ sister.
2. I have a biology class and a math class. _____ math class is boring.
2. I have a biology class and a math class. _____ math class is boring.
3. You wrote a letter to Mr. Jones on Thursday. _____ letter arrived on Friday.
3. You wrote a letter to Mr. Jones on Thursday. _____ letter arrived on Friday.

ANSWERS: 1. her (*the*) 2. My (*the*) 3. Your (*The*)

BEYOND THE RULES

The possessive apostrophe (') in 's or s' can take the place of *the* but only when used with proper nouns.

> Correct: The girl's mother is here.
> Correct: Mary's mother is here. (*Mary* is a proper noun.)
>
> Incorrect: Girl's mother is here. (*Girl* is not a proper noun.)

All except one of the highlighted nouns in the following sentences are definite. Write *the*, *a*, or ø in the space.

1. _____ Elvis Presley's music changed the world.
2. John and Jimmy wanted to play, but _____ boys' mother wouldn't let them.
3. _____ California's redwood trees are world famous.
4. _____ redwood trees of California are world famous.
5. After I heard the band, I wanted _____ lead singer's autograph.
6. After I heard the Rolling Stones, I wanted _____ Mick Jagger's autograph.
7. I took _____ Dr. Hong's Chinese history class.
8. Smoking can be dangerous to _____ person's health.

ANSWERS: 1. ø 2. the 3. ø 4. the 5. the 6. ø 7. ø 8. a

NOTE: Only in number 8 is the highlighted noun indefinite.

All of the highlighted nouns in the following sentences are definite. Write *of* in the space if the noun is a proper noun. If not, write *of the*.

1. Most _____ America's cities are modern.
2. He was born in a small country. Many _____ country's people are poor.
3. Almost all _____ Tokyo's buildings were destroyed in the great 1923 earthquake.
4. Nebraska is an agricultural state. Much _____ state's money comes from corn production.

ANSWERS: 1. of 2. of the 3. of 4. of the

Write *of* in the space if the highlighted word is a possessive adjective. Otherwise, write *of the*.

1. Easter Island used to have many trees. Today, all _____ its trees are gone.
2. Easter Island used to have many trees. Today, all _____ island's trees are gone.
3. I saw a woman at the park with her five children. Two _____ woman's children were boys.
4. I saw a woman at the park with her five children. Two _____ her children were boys.

ANSWERS: 1. of 2. of the 3. of the 4. of

45

PUTTING IT TOGETHER

Write *of*, *of the*, or ø in the space.

1. Most _____ Jim Mead's friends attended his graduation party.
2. Some _____ my friends are throwing a party for me next week.
3. Most _____ grades that Brenda got were "A"s.
4. Because of the flooding in Mazatlan, some _____ city's streets were closed.
5. Almost all _____ candy contains a lot of sugar.

ANSWERS: 1. of 2. of 3. of the 4. of the 5. ø

BEYOND THE RULES

When writing sentences, do not capitalize the word *the* in most names unless it is the first word in the sentence.

✔ Quick Check

Check the INCORRECT sentences.

❏ 1. I want to study in The United States.
❏ 2. The Republic of Costa Rica borders Panama.
❏ 3. Lake Victoria is the source of The Nile.
❏ 4. Mrs. Crabtree attended The University of Alberta in Canada.
❏ 5. The musicians will perform at The Apollo Theater in New York.

ANSWERS: 1, 3, 4, 5 (Number 2 is correct.)

Now, write the INCORRECT sentences correctly.

1. _____
2. *The Republic of Costa Rica borders Mexico.* _____
3. _____
4. _____
5. _____

ANSWERS: 1. I want to study in the United States. 3. Lake Victoria is the source of the Nile. 4. Mrs. Crabtree attended the University of Alberta in Canada. 5. The musicians will perform at the Apollo Theater in New York.

Articles, prepositions, and conjunctions (such as *and*) <u>inside</u> a name are not capitalized.

      Example: Who founded the Society for the Prevention of Cruelty to Animals?

Write these names in the logical space using the correct capitalization.

       the fraternal order of the red red rose
       the johnson and johnson company

1. _____ is a club.

2. My mother works for _____.

ANSWERS: 1. The Fraternal Order of the Red Red Rose 2. the Johnson and Johnson Company

The first letter is <u>always</u> capitalized in the names of works of literature: books, novels, plays, stories, poems, and songs.

Write these names in the logical space using the correct capitalization.

      the call of the wild (a novel)   the yellow rose of texas (a song)
      the night of the iguana (a play)   the rime of the ancient mariner (a poem)

1. Coleridge finished writing the poem _____ in 1798.

2. I think _____ is the best short novel of all.

3. The Roundhouse Theater will present _____.

4. Who recorded _____ ?

ANSWERS: 1. *The Rime of the Ancient Mariner* 2. *The Call of the Wild* 3. *The Night of the Iguana*
         4. *The Yellow Rose of Texas*

Write the most logical name in the space using correct capitalization. Underline the titles of books and plays and enclose the names of poems and songs in quotation marks.

    NOTE: The titles of books, novels, and plays are underlined when written by hand or typewritten. (With a computer and in printed material, they are *italicized*.) The titles of poems, songs, stories, and articles are enclosed in quotation marks. ("___").

      the taming of the shrew (a play)   the wayward wind (a song)
      a narrow fellow in the grass (a poem)   for whom the bell tolls (a novel)
      the university of houston   the brooklyn bridge

1. Do you have the sheet music for _____?

2. Dickinson's poem _____ is about snakes.

3. Who has read a novel by Ernest Hemingway called _____?

4. The Drama Department will produce Shakespeare's play _____.

5. Mr. Finch graduated from _____.

6. The East River is spanned by _____.

ANSWERS: 1. "The Wayward Wind" 2. "A Narrow Fellow in the Grass" 3. <u>For Whom the Bell Tolls</u> 4. <u>The Taming of the Shrew</u> 5. the University of Houston 6. the Brooklyn Bridge

ARTICLES IN CONTEXT

Read the following story and answer the questions. Then read the story again to check your answers.

The Days of Summer

3   Shirley Green took a creative writing class at the University of Littletown and wrote a short story called "The Days of Summer." After the professor read Shirley's story, he said, "This story is not very good at all. You will never sell it to a magazine. Even the title is bad."

6   The professor gave her a copy of one of his own stories. "Read this," he said. "It will give you an idea of what a <u>good</u> short story is all about. It's my best work."

"Have you sold it?" Shirley asked.

9   She was a little embarrassed when the professor answered, "Well, no — but I will someday! Even the best stories may take years to sell."

When Shirley got home, she looked at the professor's story. "'My Deepest Love,'" she read
12 aloud. "That's a worse title than mine!"

Shirley read the story and didn't think it was very good at all. She still had confidence in her own story, so she sent "The Days of Summer" to a prestigious literary magazine. To her
15 surprise, the editors loved the story and sent her a check for 600 dollars.

Shirley didn't tell her professor about the sale. She didn't want to hurt his feelings.

What was Shirley's school?

What did Shirley write?

What did the professor think
   of Shirley's story?

What was the professor's story?

What did Shirley think of
   the professor's title?

Why did she send her story
   to the literary magazine?

What did the editors think?

Did her professor's story sell?

It was _____ University of Littletown.

She wrote a story called "_____ Days of Summer."

He didn't like _____ Shirley's story.

He didn't even like _____ title.

_____ professor's story was called "My Deepest Love."

She thought it was _____ worse title than hers.

She had _____ confidence in it.

They loved _____ story.

No, Shirley's story sold, but _____ professor's didn't.

Rule 22: Use *the* with the superlative degree.

> *The Graduate* was one of the best movies I've ever seen.
> Alaska is the biggest state in the United States of America.
> This is one of the most interesting books I've ever read.

EXERCISE E4

Write the correct article in the space. Write *the* for the superlative degree.

1. The porpoise is _____ very intelligent animal.
2. The porpoise is one of _____ most intelligent animals.
3. Spanish is _____ easy language to spell.
4. I think Spanish is _____ easiest language to spell.

ANSWERS: 1. a 2. the 3. an 4. the

BEYOND THE RULES

Possessive adjectives can also take the place of *the* in the superlative degree.

Write the most logical possessive adjective in the first space. Then write *the* in the same repeated sentence.

his   my   their

1a. I like Richard Wright's novels. I think Native Son is _____ best.
1b. I like Richard Wright's novels. I think Native Son is _____ best.
2a. They have committed many crimes, but this is _____ worst.
2b. They have committed many crimes, but this is _____ worst.
3a. I told some jokes. The one about the talking horse was _____ funniest.
3b. I told some jokes. The one about the talking horse was _____ funniest.

ANSWERS: 1a. his 1b. the 2a. their 2b. the 3a. my 3b. the

BEYOND THE RULES

The chart below shows how to write the superlative form of most adjectives. Remember, however, that some adjectives like *good* and *bad* have irregular superlative forms: *the best* and *the worst*.

Complete the chart below. Write *the* before the correct form.

ONE SYLLABLE		TWO SYLLABLES ENDING WITH 'Y'	
1. big	the biggest	7. breezy	
2. cold		8. crazy	
3. hard		9. easy	the easiest
4. hot		10. lazy	
5. large	the largest	11. wavy	
6. warm		12. windy	

TWO OR MORE SYLLABLES

13. beautiful	the most beautiful
14. difficult	
15. important	
16. intelligent	
17. patient	
18. useful	

ANSWERS: 2. the coldest 3. the hardest 4. the hottest 6. the warmest 7. the breeziest 8. the craziest 10. the laziest 11. the waviest 12. the windiest 14. the most difficult 15. the most important 16. the most intelligent 17. the most patient 18. the most useful

PUTTING IT TOGETHER

Write *the* and the correct superlative adjective form in the correct sentence.

funny   quick   wide   small   hot

1. The Amazon is one of _____ rivers in the world.
2. The airplane is _____ means of transportation.
3. Death Valley, 282 feet below the sea, is one of _____ places on earth.
4. That comedian tells _____ jokes I've ever heard.

ANSWERS: 1. the widest 2. the quickest 3. the hottest 4. the funniest

BEYOND THE RULES

When the superlative degree is used with adverbs, *the* can be used without a noun.

Write *the* and the correct superlative form of the adverb in parentheses.

> NOTE: Adverbs with <u>ly</u> are not like adjectives ending with <u>y</u>. You do NOT write <u>iest</u> for their superlative form.

> You see: Of all my friends, Gregg listens _____ .
> (patiently)

> You write: Of all my friends, Gregg listens _____<u>the most patiently</u>_____ .
> (patiently)

1. Of the three women, Sarah sings _____.
(beautifully)

2. Of all animals, the snail is _____.
(slow)

3. My secretary works _____ of all.
(efficiently)

4. Who drives _____ in your family?
(carefully)

5. The person who worked _____ was Sally Brown.
(hard)

ANSWERS: 1. the most beautifully 2. the slowest 3. the most efficiently 4. the most carefully 5. the hardest

Rule 23: Do not use *the* with the comparative degree.

> Correct: Margaret is a better student than her sister.
> Correct: My brother tells more interesting stories than I.
>
> Incorrect: Margaret is the better student than her sister.

EXERCISE E5

Write the correct article in the space. If no article is needed, write ø.

1. Masahiro Matsubara is _____ more talented baseball player than I.
2. Motorcycles are usually _____ noisier machines than cars.
3. I can't make the 7:30 flight. Can I get _____ later flight?
4. Algebra is _____ easier subject than calculus.
5. People have _____ bigger brains than most other animals.

ANSWERS: 1. a 2. ø 3. a 4. an 5. ø

BEYOND THE RULES

The chart below shows how to write the comparative form of most adjectives. Remember, however, that some adjectives like *good* and *bad* have irregular comparative forms: *better* and *worse*.

Complete the chart below.

ONE SYLLABLE			TWO SYLLABLES ENDING WITH 'Y'		
1. hard	_____	test	7. early	_____	classes
2. late	_____	flight	8. curly	_____	hair
3. wide	a wider	river	9. funny	a funnier	joke
4. tall	_____	man	10. happy	_____	person
5. quick	quicker	trips	11. angry	_____	woman
6. hot	_____	desert	12. dirty	_____	shirt

TWO OR MORE SYLLABLES		
13. difficult	a more difficult	exam
14. economical	_____	airplane
15. patient	_____	fisherman
16. prestigious	_____	college
17. talented	_____	musicians
18. expensive	_____	jewelry

ANSWERS: 1. a harder test 2. a later flight 4. a taller man 6. a hotter desert 7. earlier classes 8. curlier hair 10. a happier person 11. an angrier woman 12. a dirtier shirt 14. a more economical airplane 15. a more patient fisherman 16. a more prestigious college 17. more talented musicians 18. more expensive jewelry

Adding y to a noun can make an adjective.

Complete the following chart using articles correctly.

NOUN	ADJECTIVE	COMPARATIVE FORM	
1. wind	windy	a windier	day
2. wave	wavy	wavier	hair
3. curl	_____	_____	hair
4. salt	_____	_____	popcorn
5. ease	easy	an easier	quiz
6. breeze	_____	_____	day
7. smoke	_____	_____	room
8. spice	_____	_____	kind of food
9. dirt	_____	_____	hands
10. sand	_____	_____	beach

ANSWERS: 3. curly, curlier 4. salty, saltier 6. breezy, a breezier 7. smoky, a smokier 8. spicy, a spicier 9. dirty, dirtier 10. sandy, a sandier

PUTTING IT TOGETHER

Write the adjective form for the following nouns. Then write either the superlative or comparative form of the adjectives in the sentences. Use articles correctly.

ease	spice	noise	wave	wind
__easy__	_____	_____	_____	_____

1. Look at the trees swaying in the breeze! This is _____ day we've had all year.
2. Children often shout. They're much _____ than adults.
3. I think English is _____ language than Arabic.
4. It's usually _____ on the ocean than in the mountains.
5. Jane has _____ hair of anyone in my family.
6. Mexican food is _____ food in the world.
7. My ears hurt. This is _____ engine I've ever heard.
8. My math class is the hardest and my art class _____.
9. Thai food is much _____ than Chinese food.
10. You have _____ hair than I.

ANSWERS: spicy noisy wavy windy
1. the windiest 2. noisier 3. an easier 4. windier 5. the waviest 6. the spiciest 7. the noisiest 8. the easiest 9. spicier 10. wavier

QUIZ 7

Write an article in the space provided. If no article is needed, write ø in the space. Then check your answers in the back of the book.

1. My brother dropped out of _____ University of Colorado.
2. _____ Stanford University is in Palo Alto, California.
3. The capital of _____ South Korea is Seoul.
4. _____ Dominican Republic borders Haiti.
5. Lake Titicaca is _____ highest lake in the world.

BEYOND THE RULES

The indefinite articles *a* and *an* can sometimes appear between a noun and its adjective in the comparative that uses *as* _____ *as* (the equative comparison). The same is true of certain sentences with *too*.

Example: London is a romantic city.
London is as romantic a city as Paris.

Example: It's an expensive car to buy.
It's too expensive a car for me to buy.

Write *a*, *an*, or *ø* in the correct space.

1. This isn't as _____ good _____ party as the one we had last year.
2. This party isn't as _____ good _____ as the one we had last year.
3. It's too _____ cold _____ day to go swimming.
4. It's too _____ cold _____ to go swimming.
5. Teaching isn't as _____ easy _____ as most students think.
6. Teaching isn't as _____ easy _____ job as most students think.
7. This is too _____ heavy _____ suitcase for me too lift.
8. This is too _____ heavy _____ for me too lift.
9. Hillsdale College isn't as _____ prestigious _____ school as Princeton.
10. Hillsdale College isn't as _____ prestigious _____ as Princeton.

ANSWERS: 1. ø, a 2. ø, ø 3. ø, a 4. ø, ø 5. ø, ø 6. ø, a 7. ø, a 8. ø, ø 9. ø, a 10. ø, ø

Comprehensive Test 5

Write an article in the space provided. If no article is needed, write ø in the space. Then check your answers in the back of the book.

1. Dr. Finley has a degree from _____ University of the Americas in Mexico.

2. _____ College of Design is no longer located in Hascall Hall.

3. How long have you been in _____ US?

4. _____ University of Green Village has over 10,000 students.

5. Mr. Smith liked Johnny's essay even though _____ boy's spelling was poor.

6. Greenville is very old and many of _____ town's buildings need repair.

7. That's _____ worst movie I've ever seen!

8. _____ Bay City University is well-known for its Drama Department.

9. Muhammad Ali was one of _____ greatest boxers of all time.

10. _____ Cochise College is also known as CC.

11. _____ Miami-Dade Community College is located in Miami, Florida.

12. I'd like to have _____ newer car than this one.

13. *Of Mice and Men* isn't as thick _____ book as *Moby Dick*.

14. Venus is _____ bigger planet than Mars.

15. Today isn't as windy _____ day as it was yesterday.

16. Carlos attended _____ Conway State College.

17. After the game, I washed my shirt, but _____ dirt didn't come out.

18. Mike Ellis is ill, but he can't afford to buy _____ medicine.

19. We can buy one hundred books at ten dollars _____ copy.

20. The Sutter family lives on _____ Gila Street.

Exception to Rule 23: Use *the* with the comparative degree for double comparatives or when the adjective in a comparison is used as a noun.

The bigger they are, the harder they fall. (double comparative)
The more I study, the more I learn. (double comparative)

I have two brothers. The taller is Donald. (adjective used as a noun)
Which is the better of the two cars? (adjective used as a noun)

NOTE: The comparative is only used to compare two nouns. For three or more, use the superlative.

EXERCISE E6

The following sentences compare two nouns (people or things). The highlighted comparative forms are used as nouns. Write the correct article in the space.

1. Of the two classes I took, I thought Professor Stump's was _____ better.
2. Which of the two do you want? I'll take _____ smaller.
3. Both of my sisters are beautiful, but I think _____ more beautiful is Sarah.
4. Harold and Fred are my brothers. _____ taller is Harold and _____ shorter is Fred.
5. _____ more popular of his two books is *The Day of the Hyena*.

ANSWERS: 1. the 2. the 3. the 4. the, the 5. The

EXERCISE E7

The following are double comparatives. Write *the* in all the spaces for A, B, C, and D. Then write the letter of the double comparison that goes with each of the situations below.

A. _____ more, _____ merrier!
B. _____ bigger they are, _____ harder they fall.
C. _____ more you practice, _____ luckier you get.
D. _____ older you get, _____ less you know for sure.

1. _____ Mr. Smith was playing golf with Mr. White. Mr. White practiced golf every day. Mr. Smith never practiced. Mr. White made a terrific shot and Mr. Smith said, "I can't believe it! You're the luckiest player I've ever seen!"
2. _____ Sid Savage was a heavyweight boxer. He was going to fight Moose Thomas, who weighed 350 pounds. Sid only weighed 215 pounds, but he knocked out Moose Thomas in the first round.
3. _____ I was invited to Bruce's party, and I asked him if I could bring a friend. He said, "Of course you can. If we have a lot of people, the party will be more fun."
4. _____ When I was twenty I had political opinions and ideas about exactly what was wrong with the world. I would speak out at parties and in class. Now, I am forty, and I'm not sure what I believe, so I don't voice opinions in public anymore.

ANSWERS: A through D, *The, the* 1. C 2. B 3. A 4. D

Rule 24: Use *the* with ordinal numbers and other ranking words like *next* and *last*.

> The second semester begins in January. (ordinal number)
> I hope you enjoy the next song. (ranking word)
> The last page of the book was gone. (ranking word)

EXERCISE E8

Write the correct article in the space. If no article is needed, write ø.

1. _____ next time I have to take a test, I will study for it.
2. This is _____ second rainstorm we have had this year.
3. _____ first czar of Russia was Ivan the Terrible.
4. Who was _____ last person to use the car?
5. Could you tell me when _____ next flight to New York is?
6. _____ first time I saw her, I fell in love with her.
7. This is _____ third time that this bike has needed repair.
8. _____ last dinosaur died at the end of the Cretaceous Period.
9. What time does _____ next bus arrive?
10. December 31 is _____ last day of the year.

ANSWERS: 1. The 2. the 3. The 4. the 5. the 6. The 7. the 8. The 9. the 10. the

BEYOND THE RULES

Ordinal numbers can sometimes be used with the superlative degree.

Write the correct article in the space. If no article is needed, write ø.

1. _____ fourth largest island of Japan is Shikoku.
2. I think *Tom Sawyer* is Mark Twain's _____ second best novel after *Huck Finn*.
3. Lake Victoria is _____ second largest freshwater lake in the world.
4. The vice presidency is _____ second highest position in the US.
5. My company sells _____ third most popular candy bar in the nation.

ANSWERS: 1. The 2. ø 3. the 4. the 5. the

> NOTE: Number 2 does not take *the* because the possessive apostrophe and *s* with the proper noun *Mark Twain* takes its place.

Exception (A) to Rule 24: Do not use an article with ordinal numbers or other ranking words when listing ideas.

First, read the sentence. Next, choose an answer. Last, write your choice.
Here's what to do: First, lock the door. Second, put the key in a safe place.

EXERCISE E9

Write the correct article in the space. If no article is needed, write ø.

1. Clear the table _____ first. Then, do the dishes.
2. You should _____ first learn to type before you buy a computer.
3. Wait! We can't leave now; we have to lock the door _____ first.
4. _____ first, I put in the beef. The potatoes go in _____ last.
5. _____ first, work. _____ second, save. _____ finally, invest your money.
6. _____ first car Kurt ever owned was a Volkswagen.
7. His parents said, "_____ first, go to college! Then, get a job!"
8. _____ first, do research. Then, write. _____ finally, revise your work.
9. I turned off the lights _____ first. Then I went to bed.
10. I'll tell you what to do _____ first, _____ second, and _____ third.

ANSWERS: 1. ø 2. ø 3. ø 4. ø, ø 5. ø, ø, ø 6. The 7. ø 8. ø, ø 9. ø 10. ø, ø, ø

NOTE: In Number 6, no ideas are listed.

ARTICLES IN CONTEXT

Read the following directions for making cowboy coffee. Then read the questions and complete the answers. Then read the directions again and check your work.

How to Make Cowboy Coffee

It's easy to make coffee "the Cowboy Way." Here's how:
First, light a fire and when it has died down a little, get a two-
3 quart pan, fill it with water, and set it on the fire. Second, break
an egg and put it in the pan. Put the eggshell in too. Next, put
eight tablespoons of coffee in the pan. (Cowboys like their coffee strong.) Let it boil. When the
6 water turns dark brown, take the pan off the fire and pour a little cold water in the pan. This
will make the coffee grounds sink to the bottom of the pan. Finally, pour yourself a cup. That's
the last and best step.

What do you do first?	_____ first, you light _____ fire.
Do you use a coffee pot?	No, you use _____ two-quart pan.
Where do you put the pan?	On _____ fire
What do you put in the pan?	You put _____ water, _____ coffee, and _____ egg in _____ pan.
Do you use the whole egg?	Yes, even _____ shell.
After that, what do you do?	_____ next, you put in the coffee.
Why do you put cold water in the pan?	To make _____ coffee grounds sink
Finally, what do you do?	_____ finally, you pour a cup. That's _____ last step.

Exception (B) to Rule 24: Do not use *the* with ordinal numbers when referring to names of prizes.

First prize in the Olympics is a gold medal.
Olga won second prize in the competition.

EXERCISE E10

Write the correct article in the space. If no article is needed, write ø.

1. _____ First Prize is the highest award that you can get in this contest.
2. _____ Fourth Prize is another name for_____ Honorable Mention.
3. Thank you! This is _____ first prize that I have ever won.
4. I'm not disappointed at all; _____ Second Prize is good enough for me.

ANSWERS: 1. ø 2. ø, ø 3. the 4. ø

NOTE: Number 3 does not contain the *name* of a prize.

PUTTING IT TOGETHER

Write the correct article in the space. If no article is needed, write ø.

The Unlucky Winner

Brenda told her friend Doug: "I entered _____ essay in the National Literary Contest. I was
                                              1
surprised and pleased when I won _____ First Prize. I was confident that I could win _____ First
                                      2   3
Prize again, so I immediately wrote another essay and entered it in _____ next contest. I was a
                                                                         4
little disappointed when I won _____ Second Prize. _____ third essay that I wrote won _____
                                    5   6   7
Third Prize."

Doug replied: "Let me get this straight. _____ first prize that you won was _____ First Prize,
                                              8   9
_____ second prize that you won was _____ Second Prize, and _____ third prize that you won
  10   11   12
was _____ Third Prize?"
      13

"That's right." said Brenda. "Now I've just received the results from the latest contest."

"Did you win _____ prize?" asked Doug.
                  14

"Yes," Brenda answered. "_____ Honorable Mention."
                             15

ANSWERS: 1. an 2. ø 3. ø 4. the 5. ø 6. The 7. ø 8. The 9. ø 10. the 11. ø 12. the 13. ø 14. a 15. ø

Exception (C) to Rule 24: Do not use *the* with *next* or *last* when they refer to specific times like *next month, last Christmas, next Tuesday,* and *last year.*

> Next month, I'll travel to Rome.
> Last Christmas, I bought my sister a watch.
> I'll see you next week.
> Last year I worked in a bakery.

EXERCISE E11

The following exercise illustrates how *next* and *last* can be more specific than *the next* and *the last* when used to refer to days, months, years, and holidays.

A. The correct year is not really 1990, but pretend it is 1990.

1. In 1990 "last year" means what year? _____

2. In 1990 "next year" means what year? _____

3. It is 1990. You say, "I'll visit Europe next year." In what year will you go to Europe? _____

4. It is 1990. You say, "Last year I spent the summer in Greece."

   In what year did you spend the summer in Greece? _____

ANSWERS: 1. 1989 2. 1991 3. 1991 4. 1989

B. Pretend it is 1990. In 1990, the last year and the next year can mean any year depending on the circumstances.

1. In 1990, you write: "My family and I went to Jamaica in 1985. The next year, we visited Fiji."
   In what year did you and your family visit Fiji? _____

2. In 1990, Pat said, "I came here in 1981, and the next year I went home."
   In what year did Pat go home? _____

3. It is 1990. The weatherman says, "The last year that it snowed was three years ago."
   In what year did it last snow? _____

4. The Castillos moved to California in 1957 and left the next year.
   In what year did the Castillos leave California? _____

ANSWERS: 1. 1986 2. 1982 3. 1987 4. 1958

PUTTING IT TOGETHER

Write *the* or ø in the space.

1. _____ next month I'm going to buy a new car.

2. In May of 1967, I bought a new car. I sold it _____ next month

3. _____ next year Mr. Martinez will write a book.

4. In 1988 Mr. Glenn wrote a book, and _____ next year he wrote another.

5. I'll see you _____ next week.

6. I saw you on the week of August 15. _____ next week I saw you again.

7. I will get lots of gifts _____ next Christmas.

8. I got one gift on Christmas in 1991, and _____ next Christmas I got two.

9. There was a flood _____ last week in Iowa.

10. I was sick on Monday, but _____ next day I felt much better.

11. _____ next December 31, we'll have a big New Year's Eve party.

12. In the summer of 1986 we went to Germany, and _____ next summer we went to France.

13. We hope to see you at Camp Chihuahua _____ next summer!

14. The cowboy rode into the town and left early _____ next morning.

15. I'll graduate from college _____ next year.

16. It snowed _____ last Christmas.

17. _____ next Wednesday will be our 10th wedding anniversary.

18. The company did well in 1983, but _____ next year it went out of business.

19. The first time Yoko took the TOEFL test, she scored only 467, but _____ next time she scored 500.

20. On August 1 Nancy graduated, and _____ next week she got a good job.

ANSWERS: 1. ø 2. the 3. ø 4. the 5. ø 6. The 7. ø 8. the 9. ø 10. the 11. ø 12. the 13. ø 14. the 15. ø 16. ø 17. ø 18. the 19. the 20. the

ARTICLES IN CONTEXT

Read the following anecdote that Buddy Clark told to some friends. Complete the answers to the questions below. Then read the anecdote again to check your answers.

Buddy's Funny Anecdote

"My cousin Ralph was always late for everything. He
never had any idea of what time it was. This was bothering
3   everyone in the family, so last Christmas I bought him a
watch. On Christmas day I went over and gave him the
watch and he loved it. Well, the next week I got a call from
6   him. He said, 'Why don't you come over next Saturday?' So
we made our plans and the next Saturday I drove over.
There was a lot of traffic and I had a little trouble finding his
9   place again. I knocked on the door and Ralph answered it,
but he wasn't smiling. He let me in, but he wouldn't even speak to me. He was really angry and
I didn't know why. Finally, I said, 'What's the matter?' And he looked at me and frowned.
12   'Don't you know?' I replied, 'I have no idea!' Ralph pointed to the watch I had given to him.
'You're five minutes late!' he yelled. Next Christmas, I don't think I'll get him anything."

When did Buddy give Ralph a gift?	_____ last Christmas
What was the gift?	It was _____ watch.
Why did Buddy see Ralph on Christmas?	To give him _____ watch
When did Buddy get a call from Ralph?	_____ next week
What did Ralph say on the phone?	"Come over _____ next Saturday."
When did Buddy drive over?	_____ next Saturday
What did Ralph point at?	He pointed to _____ watch.
What will happen next Christmas?	_____ next Christmas Buddy won't get Ralph a gift.

Comprehensive Test 6

Write an article in the space provided. If no article is needed, write ø in the space. Then check your answers in the back of the book.

1. Borneo is _____ third largest island in the world.

2. Don't drop that class; talk to the professor _____ first.

3. I introduced Al and Penny, and they got married _____ next day.

4. It rained on July 1st, and _____ next day it snowed.

5. Ladies and gentlemen, please welcome _____ next singer: Ranger Joe!

6. Sharon wasn't at home when I went over last Thursday, so I went back _____ next day.

7. _____ easier a test is, the happier I am.

8. _____ first class I have in the morning is algebra.

9. _____ more I eat Thai food, the more I like it.

10. I watched _____ exciting TV program last night.

11. _____ policeman directing traffic over there is going to retire next year.

12. _____ more expensive of my two cars is in the shop.

13. Wait; put the potatoes in _____ last.

14. We all hope to see you again _____ next year.

15. What did you do over summer vacation _____ last year?

16. What was _____ last movie you saw?

17. Who won _____ First Prize?

18. Why don't you come by _____ next weekend?

19. Which is _____ better of the two dishes?

20. _____ snakes are hated and feared.

CHAPTER FOUR

Part F

Read the rules for Part F and study the examples. Do not try to memorize the rules. Instead, do the exercises that follow the rules.

> **Rule 25:** Use *the* when generalizing about an entire class of musical instruments.
>
> He was a student of the trumpet. (Not any trumpet; the entire class of trumpets)
> The history of the piano is an interesting one. (the entire class of pianos)

EXERCISE F1

Write *the* or ø in the space.

1. _____ piano is perhaps the most popular instrument.
2. One could study _____ violin for a lifetime.
3. _____ clarinet is an important instrument in jazz.
4. Who invented _____ banjo?
5. Are _____ pianos very expensive?

ANSWERS: 1. The 2. the 3. The 4. the 5. ø

> NOTE: Number 5 generalizes in the plural. (See Rule 19.)

> **Exception to Rule 25:** Use *a, an,* or *the* if the sentence can mean either the general class of instrument or any particular one of the instruments. (Use *an* only before words that begin with vowel sounds.)
>
> The guitar can have six or twelve strings. (entire class)
> A guitar can have six or twelve strings. (any guitar)
> The oboe is a small instrument. (entire class)
> An oboe is a small instrument. (any oboe)

✔ Quick Check

Check the sentences that refer only to the entire class of instrument. Then write the correct articles in the spaces.

❏ 1. _____ violin is difficult to play.
❏ 2. _____ bass is a large, four-stringed instrument.
❏ 3. How many keys does _____ trumpet have?
❏ 4. I love _____ cello and all other stringed instruments.
❏ 5. I would love to learn _____ saxophone.

ANSWERS: 4, 5 (Numbers 1, 2, and 3 may refer to the entire class of instrument or any particular instrument.)
ANSWERS: 1. The or A 2. The or A 3. the or a 4. the 5. the

PUTTING IT TOGETHER

Write the correct article in the space. If no article is needed, write ø.

The Piano and the Guitar

There are several reasons why I believe that _____ piano and _____ guitar are _____ best
_____1_____ _____2_____ _____3_____

instruments that _____ person can learn to play. First of all, both are extremely popular and can
_____4_____

be found nearly everywhere. This gives a player more opportunities to enjoy _____ instruments
_____5_____

and to practice them. In addition, neither _____ guitar nor _____ piano will get in the way if you
_____6_____ _____7_____

want to sing. Have you ever seen _____ tubist sing and play—or _____ trombone player?
_____8_____ _____9_____

Whether you enjoy _____ classical music or _____ jazz is not important. All forms of music—
_____10_____ _____11_____

rock, jazz, country and classical—can easily be played on either. Studying _____ piano is _____
_____12_____ _____13_____

especially good way to understand written music because of its logically arranged keys, and a

knowledge of _____ guitar is _____ wonderful introduction to many orchestral instruments such
_____14_____ _____15_____

as_____ violin, _____ cello, and _____ bass. Indeed, if I had to start again, I would certainly
_____16_____ _____17_____ _____18_____

begin by becoming a serious student of _____ piano and _____ guitar.
_____19_____ _____20_____

ANSWERS: 1. the 2. the 3. the 4. a 5. the 6. the or a 7. the or a 8. a 9. a 10. ø 11. ø 12. the 13. an 14. the
15. a 16. the 17. the 18. the 19. the 20. the

NOTE: Numbers 6 and 7 can refer to either the general class of instrument or any particular one of the
instruments.

Rule 26: Use *the* when generalizing about an entire class of animals.

The passenger pigeon became extinct in the 20th century.
(Not just one of the pigeons became extinct but the entire class of animal.)

Humans have lived with the dog for thousands of years.
(People have not lived with only one dog but with the entire class of animal.)

EXERCISE F2

Write the correct article in the space.

1. _____ mammoth, which was very much like an elephant, became extinct at the end of the

   Pleistocene Epoch.

2. _____ cat was domesticated centuries ago.

3. Although killed in great numbers, _____ coyote has increased its range.

4. The largest land animal is _____ elephant.

5. _____ elephants are the largest land animals.

ANSWERS: 1. The 2. The 3. the 4. the 5. ø NOTE: Number 5 generalizes in the plural. (See Rule 19.)

Exception to Rule 26: Use *a, an,* or *the* if the sentence can mean either the general class of animals or any one of the animals. (Use *an* only before words that begin with vowel sounds.)

Correct:	The elephant is a large animal.	(entire class)
Correct:	An elephant is a large animal.	(any elephant)
Correct:	The coyote can live almost anywhere.	(entire class)
Correct:	A coyote can live almost anywhere.	(any coyote)

✔ Quick Check

Check the sentences that refer to only the entire class of animal. Then write the correct article in the sentence.

❏ 1. The fastest land animal is _____ cheetah.

❏ 2. _____ wolf disappeared from Europe but still lives in North America.

❏ 3. The largest animal that ever lived is _____ blue whale.

❏ 4. _____ cobra is a deadly animal.

❏ 5. _____ canary is a yellow bird that sings beautifully.

ANSWERS: Check 1, 2, 3 (Numbers 4 and 5 may refer to the entire class of animal *or* any one particular animal.)

ANSWERS: 1. the 2. The 3. the 4. The *or* A 5. The *or* A

ARTICLES IN CONTEXT

Read the following story and complete the answers to the questions. Then read the story again and check your work.

The Mountain Lion

An unusual animal lives in the Western Hemisphere—the mountain lion. It has
3   two other names: the puma and the cougar. Mountain lions live in the mountains, deserts, and forests of North America.
6   They look very dangerous. However, they rarely attack people. They usually only kill certain animals, such as rabbits and deer. A
9   mountain lion will usually try to stay away from human beings. Mountain lions are yellowish brown in color and they usually
12 weigh about 150 pounds.

Some ranchers don't like mountain lions because they sometimes eat sheep and cattle. This hurts the ranchers' business. This problem has caused a lot of political controversy
15 between the ranchers and environmentalists. The ranchers would like to hunt the mountain lions that kill their sheep and cattle. "I saw a mountain lion kill six sheep just for fun," complains Ron Bailey, a rancher in Alberta, Canada. "Something has to be done."

18 The environmentalists want to save the big cats from extinction. It is difficult for the government to serve the interests of both the ranchers and the people who want to protect these beautiful animals.

From the title, what is this story about?

What are two other names for the mountain lion?

What do mountain lions eat?

Will a mountain lion attack you?

What did Ron Bailey say?

What do the ranchers want to do?

Who are the environmentalists?

It's about _____ mountain lion.

_____ puma and _____ cougar

_____ rabbits and _____ deer

Probably not; _____ mountain lion will usually try to stay away from _____ human beings.

He said he saw _____ mountain lion kill six sheep.

They would like to hunt _____ mountain lions that kill their stock.

They're _____ people who want to protect these animals.

Rule 27: Use *the* when generalizing about an invention.

The computer has changed the world.   (The invention has changed the world — not just one computer.)

Edison invented the phonograph.   (Edison invented the entire class of the invention—not just one phonograph.)

The Aztecs used the wheel only for children's toys.   (They did not use only one wheel for toys. The sentence refers to the entire class of the invention.)

Exception to Rule 27: Use *a* or *the* if the sentence can mean either the general class of the invention or any one of the inventions. (Use *an* only before words that begin with vowel sounds.)

The phonograph reproduces natural sounds.   (invention)
A phonograph reproduces natural sounds.   (any phonograph)
The computer is useful in a small business.   (invention)
A computer is useful in a small business.   (any computer)

✔ Quick Check

Check the sentences that refer only to the entire class of invention. Then write the correct article in the space.

❑ 1. _____ satellite can make communication faster and easier.
❑ 2. _____ internal combustion engine produces carbon monoxide.
❑ 3. You can talk to people far away by using _____ telephone.
❑ 4. _____ airplane has changed the way people travel.
❑ 5. _____ transistor made it possible to build tiny radios.

ANSWERS: 4, 5 (Numbers 1, 2, and 3 may refer to the entire class of invention *or* any one of the inventions.)

ANSWERS: 1. The or A 2. The or An 3. the or a 4. The 5. The

QUIZ 8

Write an article in the space provided. If no article is needed, write ø in the space. Then check your answers in the back of the book.

1. It's not difficult to play _____ tambourine.
2. Do people really play _____ harp in heaven?
3. _____ Tasmanian wolf is almost extinct.
4. Who invented _____ wheel?
5. _____ computer can make your work easier.

Read the following story and complete the answers to the questions. Then read the story again and check your work.

The Altimeter

An altimeter is a kind of barometer that pilots use. Altimeters, like all barometers, measure the pressure of the
3   atmosphere. That is, an altimeter measures the weight of the air above it. If an airplane is at a very high altitude, the weight of the air above it is less than it would be if it were at a
6   low altitude.

It is important to understand that an altimeter does not tell the pilot how high above the ground the plane is. It tells
9   only how high above sea level the plane is flying. In Denver, Colorado, for instance, an altimeter would indicate an altitude of about one mile if the plane were sitting on the runway. This is because Denver is about one mile above sea level.

12   Another important thing to remember is that temperature and humidity affect the reading of an altimeter. Therefore, pilots must adjust the device frequently. They listen to a special channel on their radios to help them do this. Failure to adjust the altimeter could be
15   disastrous.

From the title, what is this reading about?   It's about _____ altimeter.

Who uses altimeters?   _____ pilots do.

What is an altimeter?   _____ altimeter is _____ kind of barometer.

What does an altimeter measure?   It measures _____ weight of the atmosphere.

What doesn't the altimeter tell a pilot?   It doesn't tell a pilot how high above _____ ground ___ plane is.

Why must a pilot adjust the altimeter frequently?   _____ temperature and _____ humidity can affect _____ reading of an altimeter.

Rule 28: Use *the* with the names of rivers, oceans, seas, and deserts.

The Congo River is in Africa.
The biggest ocean in the world is the Pacific.
The Sargasso Sea is located in the Atlantic Ocean.
The Mojave is a desert in the western United States.

EXERCISE F3

Write the correct article in the space.

1. Mark Twain was the pilot of _____ Mississippi River steamboat.
2. Fiji is _____ South Pacific island.
3. Who wouldn't like to sail _____ South Pacific?
4. _____ Amazon is one of the mightiest rivers on earth.
5. _____ Gobi Desert is located in Mongolia.
6. Jamaica is an island in _____ Caribbean Sea.

ANSWERS: 1. a 2. a 3. the 4. The 5. The 6. the

> NOTE: In number 1 the name of the river is used as an adjective. In number 2 the name of the ocean is used as an adjective.

Rule 29: Use *the* with plural names.

The Johnsons bought a new car last week.
The Beatles were a famous musical quartet.
The Rocky Mountains are in the western United States.
The Aleutian Islands are a part of the state of Alaska.
The Great Lakes are huge freshwater bodies of water.

EXERCISE F4

Write the correct article in the space.

1. _____ Judds are a popular mother/daughter singing team.
2. _____ Andes Mountains are in South America.
3. _____ Rockefellers are a famous and wealthy family.
4. _____ Hawaiian Islands are part of the United States.
5. My favorite baseball team is _____ New York Yankees.
6. I climbed to the top of _____ Smokey Mountain.
7. One of the most beautiful lakes in the world is _____ Lake Tahoe.
8. _____ Easter Island is a possession of Chile.

ANSWERS: 1. The 2. The 3. The 4. The 5. the 6. ø 7. ø 8. ø

> NOTE: Numbers 6, 7, and 8 do not contain plural names.

Write the correct article in the space. Then use the clues to match the number on the map with the geographic name.

AFRICA

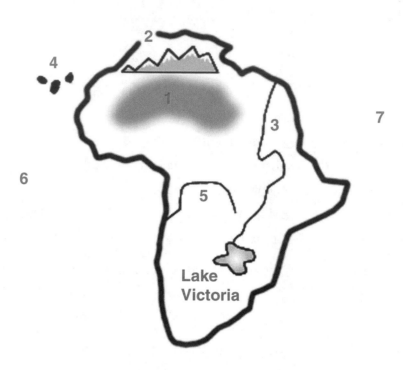

Geographical Name	Map Number	Clue
A. __the__ Nile River	__3__	flows north
B. _____ Canary Islands	_____	off Africa's NW coast
C. _____ Congo River	_____	runs west to the Atlantic
D. _____ Atlas Mountains	_____	a northern range
E. _____ Indian Ocean	_____	the ocean to the east of Africa
F. _____ Sahara Desert	_____	south of the Atlas Mountains
G. _____ Atlantic Ocean	_____	lies to the west of Africa

ANSWERS: B. the, 4 C. the, 5 D. the, 2 E. the, 7 F. the, 1 G. the, 6

Rule 30: Use *the* with family names followed by a noun.

> The Rodriquez family bought a house on Cherry Lane.
> The Everly Brothers were a famous musical duet.

EXERCISE F6

Write the correct article in the space.

1. _____ Wright brothers invented the airplane.
2. Tim Kale and Ron Stein had an accident. _____ Stein boy was hurt in the accident.
3. I met _____ Matsubara family when I visited Sapporo, Japan.

ANSWERS: 1. The 2. The 3. the

ARTICLES IN CONTEXT

Read the following story and complete the answers to the questions. Then read the story again to check your answers.

Two Brothers Get a Movie Contract

   Two high school freshmen, Mark and Danny Nelson, have
been offered a contract from a major Hollywood movie production
3 company for a screenplay that they wrote. The screenplay is a
spooky murder mystery, called "The Ghost of the Red River."

   "I always had faith in their work," says Rhonda Matlock, a
6 classmate and friend of the Nelson boys. Matlock constantly
encouraged the boys to submit their work to the movie company.
"That screenplay would still be lying in a drawer if it weren't for
9 the Matlock girl," says Mrs. Nelson. "The boys owe her a lot."
The Nelson family is now eagerly awaiting June 15 when the
movie is expected to be released.

Who wrote the screenplay?   _____ Nelson boys did.

Who is Rhonda Matlock?   _____ classmate of the boys

Why did she encourage the boys?   She had _____ faith in their work.

To whom does Mrs. Nelson give credit?   To _____ Matlock girl

Who is looking forward to June 15?   _____ Nelson family is.

Why?   That's when _____ movie will be released.

Comprehensive Test 7

Write an article in the space provided. If no article is needed, write ø in the space. Then check your answers in the back of the book.

1. At Fort Pierre, South Dakota, _____ Missouri River is dammed.

2. Buddy Holly formed a musical group called _____ Crickets.

3. _____ Urals are a major range of mountains in Europe.

4. For centuries people have used _____ horse as a beast of burden.

5. _____ cotton gin, a device for removing seeds from cotton, was an important invention.

6. In the Navy, Gregg was stationed in _____ Aleutians, a chain of Alaskan islands.

7. _____ wheel is circular in shape.

8. Mary's favorite baseball team is _____ Orioles.

9. My uncle used to be _____ New York taxi cab driver.

10. One of the most famous deserts is _____ Sahara.

11. Robert Manry crossed _____ Atlantic in a tiny boat called "the Tinkerbelle."

12. There was a fire in _____ 32nd Street cafe last night.

13. _____ Smiths have noisy neighbors.

14. After he won the lottery, he didn't know what to do _____ next.

15. Kim called and asked me to visit, so _____ next day I did.

16. _____ Lennon sisters sang beautiful harmonies.

17. The tallest animal is _____ giraffe.

18. _____ giraffes are very tall.

19. _____ giraffe is taller than an elephant.

20. _____ Idaho, one of the fifty US states, is famous for its potatoes.

CHAPTER FIVE

Part G

Read the rules for Part G and study the examples. Do not try to memorize the rules. Instead, do the exercises that follow the rules.

Rule 31: Do not use an article for the names of single lakes, mountains, islands, or canyons.

> Correct: Lake Baikal is the deepest lake in the world.
> Correct: The geology class will travel to Red Mountain.
> Correct: In Sycamore Canyon, there are several gold mines.
> Correct: Tonga is an island in the South Pacific.
> Incorrect: The Lake Baikal is the deepest lake in the world.

✔ Quick Check

Check the sentences that contain the names of lakes rather than rivers.

❏ 1. We went boating on Windermere last summer.
❏ 2. Our cabin is right next to the Gila.
❏ 3. Which is higher in altitude, Titicaca or Superior?
❏ 4. Where is the Rhine?
❏ 5. The Yangtze is 3,100 miles long.

ANSWERS: 1 and 3.

> NOTE: The others can't be lakes because of the article *the*. (See Rule 28.)

EXERCISE G1

Write the correct article in the space. If no article is needed, write ø.

1. _____ Devil's Canyon is a dangerous place to hike.
2. Mr. Pipgrass retired in a cabin on _____ Lake Minnetonka.
3. One of the most beautiful rivers in the world is _____ Snake.
4. Only a few people have climbed _____ Mt. Everest.
5. _____ Pitcairn is an island located in the Pacific Ocean.
6. _____ Sunda Islands are in the Malay Archipegalo.

ANSWERS: 1. ø 2. ø 3. the 4. ø 5. ø 6. The

> NOTE: The Sunda Islands is a plural name.

PUTTING IT TOGETHER

Write the correct article in the space. Then use the clues to match the number on the map with the geographic name.

Geographical Name	Map Number	Clue
A. <u>the</u> South China Sea	<u>3</u>	to the north of Borneo
B. _____ Krakatoa	_____	an island west of Java
C. _____ Mount Kinabalu	_____	Borneo's highest peak
D. _____ Java Sea	_____	to the south of Borneo
E. _____ Lake Toba	_____	on Sumatra
F. _____ Barito River	_____	navigable waterway in Borneo
G. _____ Barisan Mountains	_____	Sumatra's coastal range

ANSWERS: B. ø, 5 C. ø, 2 D. the, 4 E. ø, 6 F. the, 7 G. the, 1

PUTTING IT TOGETHER

Write the correct article in the space. If no article is needed, write ø.

Treasure Mountain

On the shore of _____ Lake Sawyer, there is _____ mountain. I call it _____ Treasure
1   2   3

Mountain. When I was _____ young man, I used to hike there alone. One day in June while I
4

was hiking, it began to rain. _____ terrific storm moved in very quickly, and I was quite worried.
5

It was blowing like mad, trees were bending over, and lightning was crashing all around me.

After wandering aimlessly for several hours, I found _____ cave in _____ side of _____
6   7   8

mountain. _____ cave was about five feet high and 100 yards in depth. It was _____ good
9   10

protection from _____ storm. I was cold, wet, and miserable so I went far into _____ back of
11   12

_____ cave and lighted _____ match. To my surprise, I saw _____ large wooden chest with
13   14   15

_____ strong iron lock. _____ lock was too thick for me to break, and _____ chest was too
16   17   18

heavy for me to carry. I thought about what might be in _____ chest. Could there be _____
19   20

jewels or _____ golden coins inside? I was so excited that I couldn't sleep. In _____ morning, I
21   22

left and found my way home. I promised myself to return with tools to open _____ chest and get
23

_____ treasure.
24

I have tried keep that promise. Every summer for 20 years I have gone back alone to _____
25

Treasure Mountain. However, I have failed to find _____ cave. Sometimes life is too cruel to
26

believe!

ANSWERS: 1. ø 2. a 3. ø 4. a 5. A 6. a 7. the 8. the 9. The 10. ø 11. the 12. the 13. the 14. a 15. a 16. a
17. The 18. the 19. the 20. ø 21. ø 22. the 23. the 24. the 25. ø 26. the

Rule 32: Use *the* with the names of hotels, motels, theaters, bridges, and buildings.

The Hilton Hotel is located on Main Street.
We stayed at the Philmore Motel.
The Valley Art is a theater downtown.
The Golden Gate is one of the most beautiful bridges in the world.
Class will be held in the Social Science Building.

EXERCISE G2

Write the correct article in the space. If no article is needed, write ø.

1. A famous sight in Honshu-Shikoku, Japan is _____ Ikuchi Bridge.
2. Dr. Potter's office is in _____ Fine Arts Building.
3. _____ Apollo is a famous New York theater.
4. _____ Bates Motel is a bad place to stay.
5. The conference will be held at _____ Regis Hotel.

ANSWERS: 1. the 2. the 3. The 4. The 5. the

Exception to Rule 32: Do not use an article with the names of halls or hospitals.

My dormitory is named Johnson Hall.
I was born in Hillsdale Hospital.

PUTTING IT TOGETHER

Write the correct article in the space. If no article is needed, write ø.

1. _____ Bijou, a popular movie theater downtown, has been closed for renovations.
2. My office is in _____ Irish Hall.
3. The victim was taken to _____ St Joseph's Hospital.
4. _____ Murphy Hall is the newest building on campus.
5. A new wing is being added to _____ Good Samaritan Hospital.

ANSWERS: 1. The 2. ø 3. ø 4. ø 5. ø

Rule 33: Use *the* with the names of zoos, gardens, museums, institutes, and companies.

Many people say that the San Diego Zoo is the best zoo in the world.

> The Desert Botanical Gardens is a wonderful place to spend an afternoon.
> The Natural History Museum in New York has spectacular exhibits.
> The Bradley Institute is a business school.
> The Ford Motor Company was founded by Henry Ford.

EXERCISE G3

Write the correct article in the space. If no article is needed, write ø.

1. _____ Hanging Gardens of Babylon were among the seven wonders of the ancient world.
2. _____ Geology Museum is open from 10:00 to 5:00 on weekdays.
3. _____ Westinghouse Company makes household appliances.
4. Louis Bamberger founded _____ Institute for Advanced Study in 1930.
5. _____ San Diego Zoo is one of my favorite places to spend an afternoon.

ANSWERS: 1. The 2. The 3. The 4. the 5. The

PUTTING IT TOGETHER

Write the correct article in each space. If no article is needed, write ø.

The Town of Hemstead

ANSWERS from left to right: the George Clark Zoo, the Green River, Gray Mountain, the Hemstead Bridge, the Supreme Cola Company, the Benson Hotel, Wallace Lake, Mercy Hospital, Diablo Canyon

Rule 34: Use *the* when the noun refers to something that is the only one that exists.

The sun is only a small object in the galaxy.
The pressure of the air is about 14.7 pounds per square inch.
The sky is blue.
The stars are much farther from us than the moon.
Ecuador is located on the equator.

EXERCISE G4

Write the correct article in the space. If no article is needed, write ø.

1. A satellite will begin to burn up when it reenters _____ atmosphere.
2. Do you think that _____ moon can influence people's behavior?
3. Our galaxy is only one of billions in _____ universe.
4. The hummingbird is the smallest bird in _____ world.
5. _____ Western Hemisphere is also known as the New World.

ANSWERS: 1. the 2. the 3. the 4. the 5. The

Rule 35: Use *the* to express the plural of nationalities that have no other plural form.

The French produce excellent wine.
The British defeated Napoleon at Waterloo in Belgium.
The Japanese enjoy both western and eastern music.

EXERCISE G5

Write the correct article in the space. If no article is needed, write ø.

1. _____ French are famous for their food.
2. Many visitors say that _____ Americans are friendly.
3. _____ Mexicans are fond of spicy food.
4. _____ Chinese invented paper and gunpowder.
5. _____ Burmese share a border with _____ Chinese.

ANSWERS: 1. The 2. ø 3. ø 4. The 5. The, the

PUTTING IT TOGETHER

Write the letter of the INCORRECT part of the sentence. Then write the underlined part the correct way.

INCORRECT: SHOULD BE:

1. __C__ _____the air_____   The Chinese launched a rocket that exploded in air.
                                         A   B   C

2. _____ _____   British enjoy soccer and so do the French.
                                    A   B   C

3. _____ _____   One of the best trips we had was the one to New York Zoo.
                                        A   B   C

4. _____ _____   Japanese manufacture automobiles and other products.
                                    A   B   C

5. _____ _____   Green River flows through areas of Dinosaur National Park.
                                A   B   C

ANSWERS: 2. A., The British 3. C, the New York Zoo 4. A, The Japanese 5. A, The Green River

PART H

Rule 36: Use *the* with abstract adjectives (adjectives that act as nouns to describe a group of people).

The poor need the help of the government.
The deaf sometimes use hearing ear dogs.
The disadvantaged are receiving help from local charities.
Our church feeds the hungry.

EXERCISE H1

Write the correct article in the space. If no article is needed, write ø.

1. Braille was invented to help _____ blind.

2. _____ unlucky never win at cards.

3. _____ needy should be helped.

4. _____ needy people should be helped.

5. _____ strong survive and _____ weak die.

ANSWERS: 1. the 2. The 3. The 4. ø 5. The, the

NOTE: Number 4 generalizes in the plural. (See Rule 19.)

Rule 37: **Do not use an article for the names of stadiums, malls, or parks.**

Correct: Shea Stadium can seat thousands of people.
Correct: There is a huge fountain in the middle of Sunshine Mall.
Correct: We had a picnic at Kiwanis Park.

Incorrect: The Shea Stadium can seat thousands of people.

EXERCISE H2

Write the correct article in the space. If no article is needed, write ø.

1. _____ Yellowstone Park is the most famous park in the US.
2. _____ Diablo Stadium cost four million dollars to build.
3. _____ Fiesta Mall is a great place to shop.

ANSWERS: 1. ø 2. ø 3. ø

PUTTING IT TOGETHER

Read the sentence. In the space, write the letter of the INCORRECT part of the sentence. Then write the highlighted part the correct way.

INCORRECT: SHOULD BE:

1. _A_ _The educated_ Educated can more easily get jobs than others.
            A   B   C

2. _____ _____ Equator is an imaginary line around the earth.
            A   B   C

3. _____ _____ We're having a picnic at the Ferris Park next week.
              A   B   C

4. _____ _____ People should give jobs to handicapped.
            A   B   C

5. _____ _____ The largest lake in Japan is the Biwa.
             A   B   C

ANSWERS: 2. A, The equator 3. B, Ferris Park 4. C, the handicapped 5. C, Biwa

Rule 38: Do not use an article with the names of languages or religions that have not been made definite.

Correct: Spanish is spoken in most Latin American countries.
Correct: Buddhism is practiced by millions of people.

Incorrect: The Spanish is spoken in most Latin American countries.

EXERCISE H3

Write the correct article in the space. If no article is needed, write ø.

1. _____ Arabic is spoken in the Middle East.
2. _____ Italian is a romance language.
3. _____ Urdu is the official language of Pakistan.

ANSWERS: 1. ø 2. ø 3. ø

BEYOND THE RULES

Write *the* in the space if the name of a language or religion has been made definite by an adjective clause, an adjective phrase, or a prepositional phrase. If not, write ø.

1. _____ English spoken in America is only a little different from British English.
2. _____ English is the most widespread language.
3. _____ French that Canadians speak is somewhat different from _____ French used in France.
4. _____ English of Shakespeare's time was quite different from _____ English of today.
5. _____ Spanish in the movie I saw last week was poorly pronounced.

ANSWERS : 1. The 2. ø 3. The, the 4. The, the 5. The

Exception to Rule 38: Use *the* when the word *language* is used right after the name of the language or when the word *religion* is used after the adjective for (or name of) the religion.

The English language has words from many other languages.
The Shinto religion is a native religion of Japan.

✔ Quick Check

Check the sentence if the word *language* is used after the name of a language or if the word *religion* is used after the adjective for (or name of) a religion.

❑ 1. Many wonderful works of literature are written in the Spanish language.
❑ 2. Spanish is a very popular language for American college students.
❑ 3. The Hindu religion is one of the world's oldest.
❑ 4. Hinduism is widely practiced in India.

ANSWERS: 1 and 3.

Rule 39: Do not use an article with the words *few* or *little* if the meaning is especially negative.

Correct: I'm sorry; I have few ideas.
Correct: She can't stay here very long because she has little time.

Incorrect: I'm sorry that I can't be of help; I have a few ideas.

Rule 40: Use *a* when the words *few* or *little* express a positive meaning.

Correct: He knows the subject because he has taken a few classes in it.
Correct: I want to have a little fun.

EXERCISE H4

Write the correct article in the space. If no article is needed, write ø.

1. Life was hard for me as a youth, and I had _____ few good childhood experiences.
2. Most of the records about the criminal were lost, so the police have _____ little information about him.
3. I can buy new shoes today because I have _____ little extra money.
4. Shirley is never lonely because she has quite _____ few friends.
5. The judge had _____ little sympathy; he gave the criminal life imprisonment.
6. I'll talk to you later when I have _____ little extra time.

ANSWERS: 1. ø 2. ø 3. a 4. a 5. ø 6. a

Exception to Rule 40: Use *a* when the words *few* or *little* are used with the words *only* or *just*.

I have only a few friends.   (Negative meaning)
There is just a little time.   (Negative meaning)

EXERCISE H5

Write the correct article in the space. If no article is needed, write ø.

1. Only _____ few students failed the test.
2. I don't understand much English — just _____ little.
3. There are _____ few if any good reasons to criticize others.
4. He tried to make good grades but had _____ little success.

ANSWERS: 1. a 2. a 3. ø 4. ø

✔ Quick Check

Check the sentences if the word *few* or *little* expresses a negative idea.

❏ 1. Few people live near the Arctic Ocean.
❏ 2. Samuel is lonely because he has few friends.
❏ 3. Let's sing a few songs!
❏ 4. Let's have a little fun!

ANSWERS: 1 and 2

QUIZ 9

Write an article in the space provided. If no article is needed, write ø in the space. Then check your answers in the back of the book.

1. _____ Filipino (based on Tagalog) is the native language of the Phillipines.
2. Many fossil shark teeth have been found in _____ Coal Canyon.
3. _____ British enjoy reading about their royal family.
4. _____ Chapultepec Park is located in Mexico City.
5. Be quiet! You're noisy enough to wake _____ dead!

ARTICLES IN CONTEXT

Read the following story and answer the questions. Then read the story again and check your work.

Peking Man

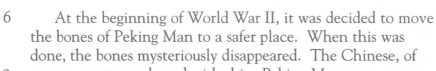

In 1926, scientists began to uncover bones in a cave near Peking, China. The bones were those of an early ancestor of
3   man, who at first was called "Peking Man." Peking Man was about five feet tall and heavily built. He knew fire and made tools.

6   At the beginning of World War II, it was decided to move the bones of Peking Man to a safer place. When this was done, the bones mysteriously disappeared. The Chinese, of
9   course, were not pleased with this; Peking Man was something of a national treasure. In addition, few fossils of early man existed at that time and little was known about him. Luckily, the scientists had made quite a few reproductions and
12   drawings of the bones. These were used to continue the study of Peking Man.

Today, Peking Man is known as *Homo erectus*. His skeletons have been found in many sites including those near the Solo River on the island of Java and the Klasies River in Africa; and,
15   of course, those discovered in the famous African canyon, Olduvai Gorge. The oldest remains of *Homo erectus* come from a site near Lake Turkana in Kenya. They are about 1.8 million years old.

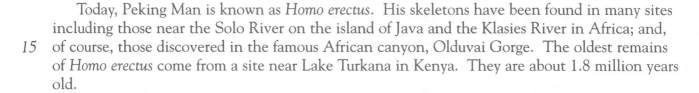

Who was Peking Man?

Is there evidence that Peking Man was smart?

What was moved for safekeeping?

What happened when the bones were moved?

Who was not pleased by this?

Were scientists pleased?

How many drawings were made of Peking Man?

Where else has Homo erectus been found?

Where was the oldest found?

_____ early ancestor of man

Yes, he knew _____ fire and made _____ tools.

_____ bones of Peking Man

_____ bones vanished.

_____ Chinese weren't pleased.

Undoubtedly not; _____ few fossils of early man had been found, and _____ little was known about him.

Luckily, quite _____ few.

Near _____ Solo River, _____ Klasies River, and in _____ Olduvai Gorge

In a site near _____ Lake Turkana

Comprehensive Test 8

Write an article in the space provided. If no article is needed, write ø in the space. Then check your answers in the back of the book.

1. I'm working nights to make _____ little extra money.

2. Because he did poorly on the first exam, Vince began to study more. However, he did _____ little better on the second exam.

3. Canadians, like Americans, speak _____ English.

4. Manila is a city in _____ Philippines.

5. _____ camera was invented in the 1800s.

6. _____ Lebanese speak Arabic.

7. I spilled _____ tomato juice on my new shirt.

8. _____ Lake Mono has very salty water.

9. _____ Mount Fuji, an extinct volcano, is the highest mountain in Japan.

10. For centuries, _____ chicken has been raised for its meat and eggs.

11. I was born in _____ Mount Sinai Hospital.

12. _____ Valley Art is the oldest theater in my hometown.

13. Countries on _____ equator are often hot and uncomfortable.

14. _____ South Mountain Park is the largest city park in the world.

15. _____ English language uses words from many other languages.

16. On December 24, it rained. _____ next day it snowed.

17. First, hypothesize. _____ second, test. Finally, evaluate.

18. _____ most Americans do not like to eat snails.

19. Many of _____ songs that Brian wrote were very good.

20. We really enjoyed _____ time we spent on Alamo Lake.

CHAPTER SIX

Read the rules for Part I and study the examples. Do not try to memorize the rules. Instead, do the exercises that follow the rules.

> **Rule 41: Use *the* for compass directions if they follow prepositions like *to, in, on, at,* or *from.***
>
> NOTE: You will notice that compass directions are often nouns when they follow prepositions. Compass directions always take *the* if they are nouns.

NOUNS:

> To the north, you can see a range of mountains.
> Europe is in the west, and Asia is in the east.
> The wind is blowing from the north.
> We are considering moving to the South.
> Manchuria is in the Far East.
> I was born in the Midwest.

ADJECTIVES:

> Taipei is in the north (northern) part of Taiwan.
> My house is on the south (southern) side of this town.
> At the north (northern) end of the city stands a tremendous tower.

> **Rule 42: Do not use an article if a compass direction <u>immediately</u> follows an action verb like *go, travel, turn, look, sail, fly, walk,* or *move.***
>
> Correct: We are considering going south next year.
> Correct: Marco Polo traveled east.
> Correct: When you get to 12th Street, turn north.
> Correct: If you look west, you can see Smokey Mountain.
>
> Incorrect: We are considering going the south next year.

✔ Quick Check

Check the sentences in which a compass direction <u>immediately</u> follows an action verb.

- ❏ 1. The airplane turned north and disappeared.
- ❏ 2. The airplane turned to the north and disappeared.
- ❏ 3. Many birds fly south for the winter.
- ❏ 4. The library is on the north side of the town.
- ❏ 5. Columbus sailed west.

ANSWERS: 1, 3, and 5

EXERCISE 11

Write the correct article in the space. If no article is needed, write ø.

1. In _____ southern part of Silver Springs, there is a residential area.
2. A shopping center can be seen on _____ western side of the town.
3. Bell Mountain is located at _____ northern end of Silver Springs.
4. The Mississippi River flows _____ south.
5. The wind usually comes from _____ west in this area.

ANSWERS: 1. the 2. the 3. the 4. ø 5. the

✔ Quick Check

Check the sentences in which a direction is a noun.

❏ 1. The Wild West was a place of danger and excitement.
❏ 2. Mr. Bergman was born in the South.
❏ 3. The Middle East has a variety of climates.
❏ 4. *Tales of the North* is a wonderful book.
❏ 5. Marco Polo traveled to the east.

ANSWERS: 1, 2, 3, 4, and 5

BEYOND THE RULES

Write the correct preposition and the article *the* in the space. (Write *in the* before *part*, *on the* before *side*, and *at the* before *end*.)

	in the	on the	at the

1. The Great Lakes are _____ northern part of the US.
2. _____ northern end of the town stands a tremendous smokestack.
3. _____ east end of the Science Building is a room with an electron microscope.
4. He was born _____ northern part of France.
5. There has been a lot of growth _____ east side of this city.

ANSWERS: 1. in the 2. At the 3. At the 4. in the 5. on the

92

BEYOND THE RULES

Left and *right* use the same article rules as compass directions.

Write the correct article in the space. If no article is needed, write ø.

1. Go north on Elm Street. The City Theater will be on _____ right.

2. Before you cross the street you should first look _____ left.

3. Driver, turn _____ right!

ANSWERS: 1. the 2. to the (or ø) 3. to the (or ø)

PUTTING IT TOGETHER

Imagine that you are a pilot flying a small airplane. Your airplane is Cesna 452. The tower is giving you instructions on the radio.

Look at your compass and complete the sentences. (Be careful; words and numbers are used a little differently on the radio.)

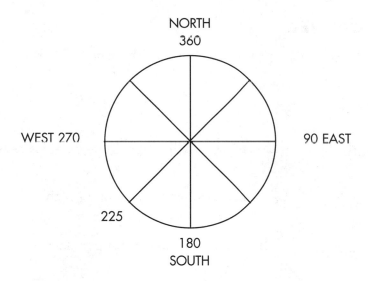

1. TOWER: *Cesna 452, turn to THREE-SIX-ZERO degrees.*

   The tower wants me to turn _____ north.

2. TOWER: *Cesna 452, you are cleared to land on runway ONE-EIGHT*

   The tower wants me to land to _____ south.

3. TOWER: *Cesna 452, do you have traffic at three o'clock?*

   The tower wants me to look _____ right.

4. TOWER: *Cesna 452, the wind is at TWO-TWO-FIVE*

   The wind is coming from _____ southwest.

ANSWERS: 1. to the (or ø) 2. the 3. to the (or ø) 4. the

Rule 43: Use *the* with large periods of historic time like the *1900's, the Jet Age, the Dark Ages, the Cambrian Period,* etc.

The Renaissance was a time of great learning.
In the Stone Age, people did not know how to use metal.
Flowering plants first appeared in the Cretaceous Period.

EXERCISE 12

Write the correct article in the space. If no article is needed, write ø.

1. Mozart wrote music in _____ late 1700's.
2. _____ Middle Ages began after the fall of the Roman Empire.
3. Do we now live in _____ Space Age or _____ Computer Age?
4. All of the dinosaurs died at the end of _____ Cretaceous Period.
5. _____ Victorian Era was named after Queen Victoria.
6. _____ 1960's were a time of rapid change.

ANSWERS: 1. the 2. The 3. the, the 4. the 5. The 6. The

PUTTING IT TOGETHER

Write the letter of the INCORRECT part of the sentence in the space. Then write the highlighted part the way it should be.

INCORRECT	SHOULD BE	
1. __C__	the western sky	Last night, a falling star streaked across western sky. A B C
2. _____	_____	A dangerous hurricane is moving the west toward Florida. A B C
3. _____	_____	The music of 1960's is still popular in much of the world. A B C
4. _____	_____	In the Bronze Age, people first mixed the copper with tin. A B C
5. _____	_____	The tall cowboy looked to west and rode off on his horse. A B C

ANSWERS: 2. B, west or to the west 3. B, the 1960's 4. B, copper 5. B, the west

BEYOND THE RULES

In Rule 13 you learned that nouns take *the* when they have been mentioned before.

Write one of the two choices in the space.

the other   **the others**

1. I have four pens. Two are blue and _____ are red.
2. I have four pens. Two are blue and _____ pens are red.
3. Fifty people called. Twenty-five were men and _____ were women.
4. There are ten books here. Eight are mine. _____ two aren't.
5. Two men robbed a bank. One of them got away and _____ didn't.

ANSWERS: 1. the others 2. the other 3. the others 4. the other 5. the other

Write one of the three words in the space.

another   **other**   **others**

1. Some dogs bite and _____ don't.
2. Many people like jazz while _____ people prefer rock and roll.
3. I have one pen here. I have _____ at home.
4. Mary's computer broke, so she bought _____ .
5. The first fire truck arrived in one minute. _____ trucks arrived later.

ANSWERS: 1. others 2. other 3. another (or others) 4. another 5. Other

Write one of the five choices in each of the spaces.

another   **other**   **others**   **the other**   **the others**

1. Humans have two favorite pets. One is the dog, and _____ is the cat.
2. Of the 20 houses on my street only two escaped the fire. _____ burned.
3. I'm taking three classes. One is easy. _____ classes are hard.
4. Kathy has two brothers in town. She has two _____ out of town.
5. Some people cried when they heard the news. _____ people laughed.
6. The coffee was delicious. Could you bring me _____ cup, please?
7. Some people watch TV, while _____ prefer to listen to the radio.
8. Some snakes lay eggs. _____ give live birth.
9. Sally wrote three books. Two were published, but _____ wasn't.
10. That spoon is dirty. Could I have _____ ?

ANSWERS: 1. the other 2. The others 3. The other 4. others 5. Other 6. another 7. others 8. Others 9. the other
         10. another

ARTICLES IN CONTEXT

Read the following story and complete the answers to the questions. Then read the story again to check your answers.

The Cambrian Explosion

3 Everyone knows that the dinosaurs became extinct at the end of the Cretaceous Period 65 million years ago. The disappearance of the dinosaurs was one of many extinctions throughout the earth's history. These
6 extinctions have fascinated scientists and laypersons alike. However, perhaps even more fascinating is a very different event — an
9 event which was really the opposite of an extinction.

12 In the early Cambrian Period, the very beginning of the Paleozoic Era, there was not an extinction but an *explosion* of life. Many new kinds of animals appeared suddenly. Some of these animals, such as snails, worms, and sponges, are familiar to us today. Others, such as the trilobite and the cystoid are now extinct. Before this "Cambrian explosion" very few kinds of
15 animals lived on the earth.

18 Why did so many new kinds of animals appear so suddenly? While there are many theories, no one knows for sure. Scientists continue to study the fossils found in Cambrian rocks in order to learn more about the great Cambrian explosion.

When did the dinosaurs become extinct?	At the end of _____ Cretaceous Period
Was the Cambrian event an extinction?	No, it was _____ explosion of life.
When was the Cambrian Period?	In _____ Paleozoic Era
Are some Cambrian animals alive today?	Some are and _____ others aren't.
Which Cambrian animals are alive today?	_____ snails, _____ worms, and _____ sponges
Which have become extinct?	_____ trilobite and _____ cystoid
Before the Cambrian explosion, how many kinds of animals lived on earth?	_____ very few
What do scientists continue to study?	_____ fossils found in Cambrian rocks

Rule 44: Do not use an article with forms of *go* in expressions such as *go to bed, goes to school, went to college, going to class, go to church, go to jail* or other multi-word verbs that have become shortened through repeated use.

Correct: I went to bed late last night.
Correct: He goes to class every day.
Correct: The minister called Mr. Brown because he wasn't going to church.
Correct: Harold has breakfast before he goes to school.
Correct: Criminals go to jail.

EXERCISE 13

Write the correct article in the space. If no article is needed, write ø.

1. Do you go to _____ church?
2. How many days a week do you go to _____ class?
3. I went to _____ school in the East.
4. If you commit a crime you may have to go to _____ jail.
5. What time did you go to _____ bed last night?

ANSWERS: 1. ø 2. ø 3. ø 4. ø 5. ø

BEYOND THE RULES

The examples in Rule 44 are only a few of the multi-word verbs that contain nouns that take no article. Consider the following sentences. They contain verbs that are similar to *go to bed, go to school, go to college, go to class, go to church,* and *go to jail.*

Cross out the article in each sentence.

1. Al Capone was sent to the jail.
2. If you want to succeed in the school, you should attend the class every day.
3. Albert left the school and went to work.

ANSWERS: 1. ~~the~~ 2. ~~the~~, ~~the~~ 3. ~~the~~

Now match the multi-word verbs on the left with their synonyms on the right by writing the correct letters in the spaces.

1. send to jail	_____	A. worship
2. go to school	_____	B. go to sleep
3. go to church	_____	C. study
4. go to bed	_____	D. imprison
5. break out of jail	_____	E. escape

ANSWERS: 1. D 2. C 3. A. 4. B 5. E

PUTTING IT TOGETHER

Write the letter of the INCORRECT part of the sentence in the space. Then write the highlighted part the way it should be.

INCORRECT   SHOULD BE

1. __B__   __bed__   Some people go to the bed early and others don't.
                                A   B   C

2. _____   _____   The judge sentenced the criminal to ten years in the prison.
                                A   B   C

3. _____   _____   I make coffee as soon as I get out of bed in morning.
                                A   B   C

4. _____   _____   The boy in the red shirt graduated from the high school.
                                A   B   C

5. _____   _____   Young person should stay in school and get an education.
                                A   B   C

ANSWERS: 2. C, prison 3. C, the morning 4. C, high school 5. A, A young person

PART J

Rule 45: Use *the* in special names, titles, and epithets.

John the Baptist was put in prison by Herod.
Skruff the Hairy One was a character in a novel.

EXERCISE J1

The following are a few examples of epithets. Write *the* in each space.

Historical Figures

Billy _____ Kid (American outlaw)

Henry _____ Fourth (King of England)

Ivan _____ Terrible (Russian Czar)

Peter _____ Great (Russian ruler)

William _____ Conqueror (Norman King of England)

Jack _____ Ripper (English murderer)

Modern Personalities

_____ Boss (Bruce Springsteen, singer)

_____ Duke (John Wayne, actor)

_____ Fab Four (the Beatles, musicians)

_____ Greatest (Muhammad Ali, boxer)

Cartoon Characters

Wendy _____ Witch

Felix _____ Cat

Caspar _____ friendly ghost

Names of Places

_____ City of Eternal Spring
      (Cuernavaca, Mexico)

_____ Lone Star State (Texas)

_____ Land of the Rising Sun (Japan)

_____ Big Apple (New York City)

Rule 46: Use *the* for body parts that have been touched by an outside object.

Sid Smith hit Johnny Johnson in the eye.
The soldier was struck in the arm by a bullet.
The politician kissed 100 babies on the forehead.

NOTE: In most other sentences, body parts take a possessive adjective like *my*, *his*, *her*, *your*, *their*, or *our*.

EXERCISE J2

Write the correct article in the space.

1. The outlaw shot the sheriff in _____ back.
2. The teacher touched me on _____ shoulder and said, "Stop writing now."
3. The baseball coach slapped Masahiro on _____ back and said, "Good work."
4. The doctor gave me an injection in _____ arm.

ANSWERS: 1. the 2. the 3. the 4. the

✔ Quick Check

Check the sentences in which a body part has been touched by an outside object.

❏ 1. I fell down and broke my arm when I was nine years old.
❏ 2. After Diana ran the race, her legs were tired.
❏ 3. When I'm embarrassed my face turns red.
❏ 4. My head aches.
❏ 5. The policeman took the criminal by the arm and led him away.

ANSWER: 5

PUTTING IT TOGETHER

Write the correct possessive adjective (*my*, *your*, *his*, *her*, etc.) in the space. If the body part has been touched by an outside object, write *the* instead.

1. Wear a helmet when you play baseball in case you get hit on _____ head by the ball.
2. I wash _____ hair every day.
3. She left the room, _____ face red with anger.
4. The ball hit Billy on _____ head.
5. Muhammad Ali hit his opponent on _____ chin.
6. After the earthquake, _____ hearts went out to the families of the victims.

ANSWERS: 1. the 2. my 3. her 4. the 5. the 6. our

Rule 47: Do not use an article with the names of diseases.

Correct: Heart disease kills millions every year.
Correct: Cancer is not a contagious disease.
Correct: Only a few decades ago, polio was a common childhood disease.

Incorrect: The heart disease kills millions every year.

Exception to Rule 47: Use *the* with *the flu, the measles,* and *the mumps*.

Influenza is also called the flu.
The measles is a childhood disease.
The mumps causes swelling of the glands.

EXERCISE J3

Write the correct article in the space. If no article is needed, write ø.

1. There are viral and bacterial forms of _____ pneumonia.
2. _____ bubonic plague is spread by a kind of flea.
3. _____ diphtheria is a childhood disease.
4. _____ mumps is more uncomfortable for adults than for children.
5. _____ influenza is also called _____ flu.
6. _____ measles can be very serious.
7. _____ Lyme disease is spread by the bite of a tick.

ANSWERS: 1. ø 2. ø 3. ø 4. The 5. ø, the 6. ø, the 7. ø

ARTICLES IN CONTEXT

Read the following story and complete the answers to the questions. Then read the story again and check your answers.

Beriberi

3 Beriberi is a disease caused by the lack of vitamin B1 (thiamine). The name comes from the Singhalese language and means "I cannot." (People stricken with beriberi are so weak that they cannot do anything.) Beriberi attacks the nervous system of its victims. The disease is common in Asian countries where white rice is a staple food. Unlike brown rice, white rice is very poor in vitamin B.

What causes beriberi?   _____ lack of vitamin B1 causes _____ beriberi.

Where does the name come from?   It comes from _____ Singhalese language.

Which kind of rice is more nutritious?   _____ brown rice is.

Rule 48: **Do not use an article when referring to numbers or letters in a list.**

Correct: Could you read number 1, please?

Correct: "B," "C," and "D" are incorrect.

Correct: In question number 5, "A" is the correct response.

Incorrect: Could you read the number 1, please?

EXERCISE J4

Write the correct article in the space. If no article is needed, write ø.

1. You'll have to retype this; there are ten mistakes on _____ page one.

2. Dr. Smith, the first word in _____ question two is hard to read.

3. In _____ number ten, _____ "A" is correct.

4. All of the statements are true except for _____ 7, which is false.

5. My name begins with _____ "L."

ANSWERS: 1. ø 2. ø 3. ø, ø 4. ø 5. an

NOTE: In number 5, the name of the letter is not in a list.

BEYOND THE RULES

In Exception A to Rule 24, you learned not to use *the* with ordinal numbers or ranking words when listing ideas.

Write ø in the space if the letter, number, ranking word, or ordinal number is a part of a list.

1. _____ first, I take a shower, and then I have breakfast.

2. Chapters _____ 1, _____ 4, and _____ 6 deal with articles.

3. After you win a gold medal in the Olympics, what do you do _____ next?

4. _____ next time I take a test, I'll be ready.

5. The teacher wrote an "X" on the blackboard. _____ "X" was two feet high.

ANSWERS: 1. ø 2. ø, ø, ø 3. ø 4. The 5. The

Rule 49: Use *the* with nouns for military institutions, such as the army, the navy, the air force, the marines, the military, as well as the fire department, the police, etc.

> He spent ten years in the army.
> At the age of eighteen, he joined the navy.
> The marines secured the beach.
> Many pilots got their training in the air force.
> His career was in the military.
> The fire department arrived in time to put out the fire.

EXERCISE J5

Write the correct article in the space. If no article is needed, write ø.

1. Some young people join _____ army to learn a trade.
2. Not everyone in _____ air force is a pilot.
3. There has been a robbery. Could someone please call _____ police?
4. _____ navy is one branch of _____ military.
5. My brother-in-law was _____ navy pilot.

ANSWERS: 1. the 2. the 3. the 4. the, the 5. a

> NOTE: In number 5, *navy* is used as an adjective.

Rule 50: Use *the* with the word *same*.

> Kathy and I got the same grade.
> Twins often have the same interests.

EXERCISE J6

Write the correct article in the space. If no article is needed, write ø.

1. My sister and I have _____ same color eyes.
2. Coca Cola is _____ same as Coke.
3. The police think that the two crimes were committed by _____ same person.
4. I drove to Arrow Lake early in the morning so that I could come back _____ same day.

ANSWERS: 1. the 2. the 3. the 4. the

ARTICLES IN CONTEXT

Read the following story and complete the answers to the questions. Then read the story again to check your answers.

Scurvy

Scurvy and beriberi are occasionally confused, but they are not the same. Scurvy, like beriberi, is caused by a vitamin deficiency, but of vitamin C, not vitamin B_1. Unlike beriberi,
3 the signs of scurvy are swelling and bleeding of the gums and sudden tooth loss. The disease was particularly common aboard ships making long voyages in the 1700's and before. Sailors used to eat very little fresh food, and their diet was very poor in vitamin C. It was not unusual for half
6 the crew to die of scurvy during long voyages.

In 1795, the British navy combated the problem by providing fresh limes to its sailors on all long voyages. The limes were rich in vitamin C and prevented the disease. Today, British sailors
9 are still called "limeys" because of this practice.

Are beriberi and scurvy the same?	No, they're not _____ same.
When was scurvy common?	during _____ 1700's and before
Which branch of the armed forces combatted scurvy in 1795?	_____ navy
What did the navy do?	_____ navy gave its sailors _____ limes.

Quiz 10

Write an article in the space provided. If no article is needed, write ø in the space. Then check your answers in the back of the book.

1. Chile is located on _____ west coast of South America.
2. The Renaissance began in _____ late 1400's.
3. Many birds fly _____ south for the winter.
4. _____ rabies is one of the most dreaded diseases.
5. Mr. Brown will not be in the office today because he has _____ flu.

Comprehensive Test 9

Write an article in the space provided. If no article is needed, write ø in the space. Then check your answers in the back of the book.

1. Where do you go to _____ school?

2. Sam threw an apple. The apple hit Bill in _____ nose.

3. _____ measles can be a very serious disease.

4. _____ typhus has sometimes killed more soldiers in wars than those who died in battle.

5. _____ Chapter Five is longer than the rest.

6. _____ late 1800's were the years of the Wild West.

7. He received an honorable discharge from _____ army.

8. Meat loaf again? We had _____ same thing for dinner last night!

9. Philip _____ Fair was a handsome man.

10. I have four dictionaries. Two are Japanese and _____ others are English.

11. To _____ east of my house is a noisy factory.

12. _____ Ice Age is divided into many periods.

13. Before you buy an expensive piano, you should _____ first learn how to play on a cheaper one.

14. In 1963, John Kennedy said he wanted men to go to the moon before _____ next decade.

15. I don't have enough credits to graduate now, so I have to wait until _____ next year.

16. _____ Hempstead Zoo will be closed for the winter.

17. I made a mistake and can't erase it. Do you have _____ pencil with an eraser?

18. Please don't walk on _____ grass in front of my house.

19. Do you need _____ people who can translate English to Tagalog?

20. I wonder what happened to _____ old camera that my grandfather used to have.

Comprehensive Test 10

This is the final test. It covers all 50 rules and 15 exceptions. Write an article in the space provided. If no article is needed, write ø in the space. Then check your answers in the back of the book.

1. Between Italy and Greece lies _____ Adriatic Seas.

2. Caroline Newman is majoring in _____ art at the university.

3. _____ Art Museum is located in the James Fisher Building.

4. Coffee in this restaurant is only 25 cents _____ cup.

5. _____ Tokyo is one of the most populous cities in the world.

6. Everyone in the class missed _____ question number 23 on the test.

7. _____ University of Greenville is a good place to study.

8. For dessert, I'd like _____ slice of that apple pie, please.

9. _____ Chinese have a long history.

10. George Rawson owns a nightclub on _____ Santa Monica Boulevard.

11. Good night, everyone. See you in _____ morning!

12. Henry Benson and Jim Smith had an accident last week. _____ Smith boy was hurt.

13. Henry won _____ second prize in the university diving contest.

14. How do you like the United States? Is this _____ first time you have been here?

15. The more I study this subject, _____ more confused I get.

16. Hurry! Hurry! We have _____ little time.

17. _____ Navajo is one of the most widely spoken Native American languages.

18. I asked the pilot how high above _____ ground we were flying.

19. I bought more sugar because we has only _____ little left.

20. I buy the cheapest brand of aspirin because they're all _____ same.

21. _____ Arrow Lake is one of the prettiest lakes I've ever seen.

22. I can't take a summer vacation right now, but _____ next year I will.

23. _____ world in which we live is constantly changing.

24. I don't have enough money right now to buy _____ new clothes.

25. I've felt weak ever since I caught _____ flu last month.

26. If anyone needs a pencil, just ask; I have _____ few extras.

27. _____ Gila monster is one of the two poisonous lizards in the world.

28. If you look into _____ north on a clear night, you will see Polaris, the North Star.

29. If you want to study physics, you will _____ first have to take several math classes.

30. In the autumn, my back yard is covered with _____ leaves.

31. Jerry Thompson did _____ excellent job while he worked for us.

32. Johnny's mother took him by _____ hand and walked him across the street.

33. Lake Baikal is located in _____ former Soviet Union.

34. Last year I took _____ wonderful art history class.

35. Mary was in _____ top ten per cent of her high school class.

36. Mastery of _____ English language is the goal of many international students.

37. _____ dog that growls will very often bite as well.

38. Most airliners can travel at 600 miles _____ hour.

39. Most birds don't fly at _____ night.

40. Mrs. Martin dropped a glass and _____ glass broke.

41. My favorite basketball team is _____ Sonics.

42. Our club is going to have a picnic at _____ Audubon Park.

43. _____ computer makes it easy to revise written work.

44. Please don't put your nose against _____ window; I just washed it.

45. _____ dog can be taught to understand many words.

46. Some people don't like _____ tomato juice.

47. Some people go to _____ church every Sunday.

48. _____ arthritis is a painful disease.

49. That actor was one of _____ Magnificent Seven in the famous film.

50. The Anthropology Department is located in _____ Hascall Hall.

51. Civil unrest in the country became so serious that _____ military was called in to control it.

52. The company has reserved a room for you at _____ Hilton Hotel.

53. _____ green plants produce oxygen.

54. The government provides support for _____ poor.

55. The invention of _____ crossbow made it possible to shoot arrows farther and more accurately.

56. _____ bugle is a trumpet-like instrument.

57. The leader of that country attended _____ Oxford University in England.

58. The prairie falcon is one of _____ fastest birds in the world.

59. The ship sailed out of the harbor and headed _____ north.

60. There are _____ vast plains in Argentina.

61. There is one musical instrument I truly love; _____ clarinet.

62. This is the first time that I've received _____ "99" on a test.

63. Vivian studied hard and got _____ "A" in her English class.

64. When did _____ Stone Age end?

65. You have _____ better accent in English than I.

# APPENDIX

Glossary

Abstract Adjective: an adjective that acts as a plural noun to describe a group of people
Examples: *the blind, the disadvantaged, the poor, the hungry, the rich*

Abstract Noun: a noun you cannot see, touch, or feel
Examples: *love, death, education, geology, hiking*

Adjective Clause: a clause with a subject and a verb that acts as an adjective to describe a person or thing

Examples: The teacher that we had last semester was especially good.
The man who hired me yesterday left the company today.
The car which the Smiths bought gets 50 miles a gallon.
The town where I grew up is now a big city.
The man she married was poor.

Adjective Phrase: a phrase without a subject and a verb that describes a person or thing

It may have the past participle of a verb (*arrested, destroyed*) or the present participle (*standing, living*)
Examples: The man arrested by the police went to jail.
The house destroyed by the fire was mine.
The woman standing by the door is my sister.
The teenagers living next door play loud music late at night.

Article: *a, an,* and *the*

Class: a group of similar things uses adjectives with *-er, -ier, more,* or *as _____ as* to compare things

Comparative Degree: an expression that uses adjectives with *-er, -ier, more,* or *as ___ as* to compare things
Examples: *colder than, faster than, easier than, more difficult than, as quick as*

Consonant: a sound or letter other than a vowel: *b, c, d, f, g, h, j, k, l, m, n, p, q, r, s t v, w, x, y, z*

Count Noun: a noun that can be counted and that has a plural form
Examples: *apple, pencil, house, sheep*

Definite: known, already understood, or already mentioned

Epithet: a description of a person or thing often beginning with the name of the person or thing
Examples: Henry the Eighth, John the Baptist

Generalize: to talk about in a general, nonspecific way

Indefinite: not known, not already understood, or not already mentioned

Known: definite, already understood, or already mentioned

Logical: sensible, making sense

Noncount Noun: a noun that has no plural and cannot be counted
Examples: *milk, air, sand*

Noun: a person or a thing

Number: referring to whether something is singular or plural
Example: The following sentences are INCORRECT because the verbs do not agree in number with the subjects. *Two men is here. A book are on the table.*

Ordinal Number: a number ending with *-st, -nd, -rd, -th,* or *-ieth*
Examples: *first, second, third, fourth, twentieth*

Per: for each, for every

Plural: more than one

Possessive Adjective: words such as *my, your, his, her, their,* and *our*

Preposition: a function word such as *of, in, on, at, to, from, before, after, over, across* and *under*

Prepositional Phrase: a group of words beginning with a preposition such as *of, in, on, at, to,* or *from*
Examples: The back of this room is dirty.
The prerequisites for this class are algebra and chemistry.
The man in the red shirt is my boss.

Proper Adjective: an adjective formed from a proper noun
Examples: *Canadian, Buddhist, Taiwanese*

Proper Noun: a noun that is a name and must be capitalized
Examples: *America, Mary, New York*

Quantity: an amount that can be measured

Ranking Words: words that show the importance or order of things
Examples: ordinal numbers, *next, last*

Referring to: talking about, having to do with

Singular: not plural, referring to only one

Specific: special, not general

Superlative Mode: an expression that uses adjectives with *-st, -iest,* or *most* to compare things
Examples: *the coldest, the fastest, the easiest, the most difficult*

There + be: *there is, there are, there was, there were, there have been, there will be,* and so on

Verb Form: a word formed from a verb that is used as another part of speech

Vowel: *a, e, i, o,* or *u*

KEY TO QUIZZES AND COMPREHENSIVE TESTS

Quizzes

Quiz 1

Answer	Rule(s)
1. an	2
2. ø	4, 5
3. a	1, 6
4. an	2
5. ø	3, 5

Quiz 2

Answer	Rule(s)
1. an	8
2. an	8
3. an	10
4. an	10
5. a	9

Quiz 3

Answer	Rule(s)
1. The	13
2. ø	4, 5
3. the	13
4. an	2
5. ø	4,5

Quiz 4

Answer	Rule(s)
1. a	1, 5, 6
2. The	15
3. a	1, Exc. c. 15
4. The	15
5. ø	

Quiz 5

Answer	Rule(s)
1. The	16
2. a	1,6, Exc. 16
3. the	15
4. The	16
5. a	1, 6, Exc. 15

Quiz 6

Answer	Rule(s)
1. ø	17
2. The	15
3. ø	19
4. ø	19
5. ø	18

Quiz 7

Answer	Rule(s)
1. the	Exc. 20
2. ø	20
3. ø	21
4. The	Exc. 21
5. the	22

Quiz 8

Answer	Rule(s)
1. the/a	Exc. 25
2. the	25
3. The	26
4. the	27
5. The/A	Exc. 27

Quiz 9

Answer	Rule(s)
1. ø	38
2. ø	31
3. The	35
4. ø	37
5. the	36

Quiz 10

Answer	Rule(s)
1. the	41
2. the	43
3. ø	42
4. ø	47
5. the	Exc. 47

Comprehensive Tests

Comp Test 1

Answer	Rule(s)
1. an	2, 6
2. ø	3, 5, 6
3. a	1
4. an	2
5. a	1
6. an	2
7. ø	3, 5
8. a	1
9. ø	4, 5
10. an	2
11. a	1
12. a	1
13. ø	4, 5
14. ø	4, 5
15. ø	4, 5
16. A	1
17. ø	4, 5
18. a	1
19. ø	4, 5
20. ø	3, 6

Comp Test 2

Answer	Rule(s)
1. an	10
2. The	13
3. a	1
4. A	1
5. An	2
6. the	14
7. The	13
8. An	8
9. the	14
10. a	7
11. the	13
12. ø	12
13. the	14
14. an	2
15. ø	4, 5
16. a	9
17. the	13
18. The	14
19. the	13
20. the	11

Comp Test 3

Answer	Rule(s)
1. ø	4, 5
2. a	1, Exc. 15
3. The	15
4. ø	3, 5
5. the	15
6. ø	3, 5
7. the	15
8. the	14
9. ø	3, 5
10. the	15
11. A	1, Exc. 5
12. The	15
13. a	1, Exc. 5
14. a	1, 6, Exc. 15
15. ø	4, 5
16. The	13
17. The	13
18. an	10
19. The	14
20. an	8

Comp Test 4

Answer	Rule(s)
1. the	16
2. ø	19
3. the	15
4. the	14
5. ø	17
6. an	2
7. the	16
8. ø	19
9. the	15
10. ø	18
11. a	1, Exc. 15
12. the	15
13. the	14
14. the	13
15. ø	18
16. ø	3, 5
17. ø	4, 5
18. a	1
19. ø	17
20. the	16

Comp Test 5

Answer	Rule(s)
1. the	Exc. 20
2. The	Exc. 20
3. the	Exc. 21
4. The	Exc. 20
5. the	13
6. the	13
7. the	22
8. ø	20
9. the	22
10. ø	20
11. ø	20
12. a	1, 23
13. a	1, 23
14. a	1, 23
15. a	1, 23
16. ø	20
17. the	14
18. ø	4, 5
19. a	9
20. ø	17

Comp Test 6

Answer	Rule(s)
1. the	22
2. ø	Exc. A 24
3. the	24
4. the	24
5. the	24
6. the	24
7. The	Exc. 23
8. The	24
9. The	Exc. 23
10. an	2
11. The	16
12. The	Exc. 23
13. ø	Exc. A 24
14. ø	Exc. C 24
15. ø	Exc. C 24
16. the	24
17. ø	Exc. B 24
18. ø	Exc. C 24
19. the	Exc. 23
20. ø	19

Comp Test 7

Answer	Rule(s)
1. the	28
2. The	29
3. The	29
4. the	26
5. The	27
6. the	29
7. The/A	Exc. 27
8. the	29
9. a	1
10. the	28
11. the	28
12. a	1
13. The	29
14. ø	Exc. A 24
15. the	24
16. The	29
17. the	26
18. ø	19
19. The/A	Exc. 26
20. ø	21

Comp Test 8

Answer	Rule(s)
1. a	40
2. ø	39
3. ø	38
4. the	29
5. The	27
6. The	35
7. ø	4, 5
8. ø	31
9. ø	31
10. the	26
11. ø	Exc. 32
12. The	32
13. the	34
14. ø	37
15. The	Exc. 38
16. The	24
17. ø	Exc. A 24
18. ø	19
19. the	16
20. the	16

Comp Test 9

Answer	Rule(s)
1. ø	44
2. the	46
3. the	Exc. 47
4. ø	47
5. ø	48
6. the	43
7. the	49
8. the	50
9. the	45
10. the	13
11. the	41
12. The	43
13. ø	Exc. A 24
14. the	24
15. ø	Exc. C 24
16. The	33
17. a	1, Exc. 15
18. the	15
19. ø	3, Exc. 16
20. the	16

Comp Test 10

Answer	Rule(s)
1. the	28
2. ø	18
3. The	33
4. a	9
5. ø	21
6. ø	48
7. The	Exc. 20
8. a	Exc. 15
9. The	35
10. ø	17
11. the	11
12. The	30
13. ø	Exc. B 24
14. the	24
15. the	Exc. 23
16. ø	39
17. ø	38
18. the	34
19. a	Exc. 40
20. the	50
21. ø	31
22. ø	Exc. C 24
23. The	16
24. ø	5, 3
25. the	47
26. a	40
27. The	26
28. the	41
29. ø	Exc. A 24
30. ø	3, 5
31. an	2, 5
32. the	46
33. the	Exc. 21
34. a	1, 5
35. the	15
36. the	Exc. 38
37. A	Exc. 16, 5
38. an	10
39. ø	12
40. the	13
41. the	29
42. ø	37
43. The/A	Exc. 27
44. the	14
45. The/A	Exc. 26
46. ø	4, 5
47. ø	44
48. ø	47
49. the	45
50. ø	Exc. 32
51. the	49
52. the	32
53. ø	19, 5, 3
54. the	36
55. the	27
56. The/A	Exc. 25
57. ø	20
58. the	22
59. ø	42
60. ø	6, 3, 5
61. the	25
62. a	7, 5
63. an	8, 5
64. the	43
65. a	23, 1, 5

RULES AND EXCEPTIONS

Comprehensive List

Rule 1: Use *a* when a singular count noun is indefinite and the article is followed by a consonant sound.

Rule 2: Use *an* when a singular count noun is indefinite and the article is followed by a vowel sound.

Rule 3: Do not use *a* or *an* with plural nouns.

Rule 4: Do not use *a* or *an* with noncount nouns.

Rule 5: Do not use *the* with indefinite nouns.

Rule 6: Do not use *the* with *there* + "be." (All nouns, plural and singular, are indefinite if they occur after *there* + "be.")

Rule 7: Use *a* for single letters and numbers that begin with a consonant sound.

Rule 8: Use *an* for letters and numbers that begin with a vowel sound.

Rule 9: Use *a* to mean "for each" or "per" when the noun begins with a consonant sound.

Rule 10: Use *an* to mean "for each" or "per" when the noun begins with a vowel sound.

Rule 11: Use *the* with *in the morning, in the afternoon,* and *in the evening.*

Rule 12: Do not use an article for *at night.*

Rule 13: Use *the* when the noun has already been mentioned.

Rule 14: Use *the* when the noun that follows is already known.

Rule 15: Use *the* when the noun is made definite by a prepositional phrase.

Exception to Rule 15: Do not use *the* when the prepositional phrase does not make the noun definite.

Rule 16: Use *the* when the noun is made definite by an adjective clause or an adjective phrase.

Exception to Rule 16: Don't use *the* when the adjective clause or adjective phrase does not make the noun definite.

Rule 17: Do not use an article with the names of streets, avenues, roads, lanes, or boulevards.

Rule 18: Do not use an article when generalizing about abstract nouns.

Rule 19: Do not use an article when generalizing in the plural.

Rule 20: Do not use an article with the names of universities or colleges.

Exception to Rule 20: Use *the* with names of colleges and universities that contain the word *of.*

Rule 21: Do not use an article with the names of countries, cities, or states.

Exception to Rule 21: Use *the* in the names of countries that contain the words *united, union, kingdom,* or *republic.*

Exception to Rule 21: Use *the* in the names of countries that contain the words *united, union, kingdom,* or *republic*.

Rule 22: Use *the* with the superlative degree.

Rule 23: Do not use *the* with the comparative degree.

Exception to Rule 23: Use *the* with the comparative degree for double comparatives or when the adjective in a comparison is used as a noun.

Rule 24: Use *the* with ordinal numbers and other ranking words like *next* and *last*.

Exception (A) to Rule 24: Do not use an article with ordinal numbers or other ranking words when listing ideas.

Exception (B) to Rule 24: Do not use *the* with ordinal numbers when referring to names of prizes.

Exception (C) to Rule 24: Do not use *the* with *next* or *last* when they refer to specific times like *next month, last Christmas, next Tuesday,* and *last year*.

Rule 25: Use *the* when generalizing about an entire class of musical instruments.

Exception to Rule 25: Use *a, an,* or *the* if the sentence can mean either the general class of instrument or any particular one of the instruments. (Use *an* only before words that begin with vowel sounds.)

Rule 26: Use *the* when generalizing about an entire class of animals.

Exception to Rule 26: Use *a, an,* or *the* if the sentence can mean either the general class of animals or any one of the animals. (Use *an* only before words that begin with vowel sounds.)

Rule 27: Use *the* when generalizing about an invention.

Exception to Rule 27: Use *a* or *the* if the sentence can mean either the general class of the invention or any one of the inventions. (Use *an* only before words that begin with vowel sounds.)

Rule 28: Use *the* with the names of rivers, oceans, seas, and deserts.

Rule 29: Use *the* with plural names.

Rule 30: Use *the* with family names followed by a noun.

Rule 31: Do not use an article for the names of single lakes, mountains, islands, or canyons.

Rule 32: Use *the* with the names of hotels, motels, theaters, bridges, and buildings.

Exception to Rule 32: Do not use an article with the names of halls or hospitals.

Rule 33: Use *the* with the names of zoos, gardens, museums, institutes, and companies.

Rule 34: Use *the* when the noun refers to something that is the only one that exists.

Rule 35: Use *the* to express the plural of nationalities that have no other plural form.

Rule 36: Use *the* with abstract adjectives (adjectives that act as nouns to describe a group of people).

Rule 37: Do not use an article for the names of stadiums, malls, or parks.

Rule 38: Do not use an article with the names of languages or religions that have not been made definite.

Exception to Rule 38: Use *the* when the word *language* is used right after the name of the language or when the word *religion* is used after the adjective for (or name of) the religion.

Rule 39: Do not use an article with the words *few* or *little* if the meaning is especially negative.

Rule 40: Use *a* when the words *few* or *little* express a positive meaning.

Exception to Rule 40: Use *a* when the words *few* or *little* are used with the words *only* or *just*.

Rule 41: Use *the* for compass directions if they follow prepositions like *to, in, on, at,* or *from.*

Rule 42: Do not use an article if a compass direction <u>immediately</u> follows an action verb like *go, travel, turn, look, sail, fly, walk,* or *move.*

Rule 43: Use *the* with large periods of historic time like the *1900's, the Jet Age, the Dark Ages, the Cambrian Period,* etc.

Rule 44: Do not use an article with forms of *go* in expressions such as *go to bed, goes to school, went to college, going to class, go to church, go to jail* or other multi-word verbs that have become shortened through repeated use.

Rule 45: Use *the* in special names, titles, and epithets.

Rule 46: Use *the* for body parts that have been touched by an outside object.

Rule 47: Do not use an article with the names of diseases.

Exception to Rule 47: Use *the* with *the flu, the measles,* and *the mumps.*

Rule 48: Do not use an article when referring to numbers or letters in a list.

Rule 49: Use *the* with nouns for military institutions, such as the army, the navy, the air force, the marines, the military, as well as the fire department, the police, etc.

Rule 50: Use *the* with the word *same.*

DATE